Gen Z Misunderstood

Gen Z Misunderstood

Changing the Narrative
on Today's Misfits and Dreamers

TANNER CALLISON

WIPF & STOCK · Eugene, Oregon

GEN Z MISUNDERSTOOD
Changing the Narrative on Today's Misfits and Dreamers

Wipf & Stock
An Imprint of Wipf and Stock Publishers
199 W. 8th Ave., Suite 3
Eugene, OR 97401

www.wipfandstock.com

PAPERBACK ISBN: 978-1-6667-4355-5
HARDCOVER ISBN: 978-1-6667-4356-2
EBOOK ISBN: 978-1-6667-4357-9

JUNE 8, 2022 3:08 PM

Dedicated to: Amber, my wife, my friend,
and my partner in mobilizing this generation.

Contents

Acknowledgments

I AM INDEBTED TO many friends, mentors, coworkers, and colaborers in the gospel.

First and foremost, I owe my all the triune God. He is the covenant Lord of history who came, lived, and died to give new life. Apart from his saving grace, I would be a wandering sheep, but he brought me into his fold and promises to keep me.

I thank The Traveling Team and many coworkers and colaborers in mobilization over the last eight years. I thank Claude Hickman for hiring me and believing in my crazy ideas along the way. He contributed many ideas to this book. I'm thankful for the many teammates who loved me and challenged me to be a better man of God. The Traveling Team has allowed me a front-row seat to what God is doing among Gen Z.

I'm thankful for Todd Ahrend, who met me as a dopey college freshman and challenged me to love Jesus and understand his heart for all nations. Todd mentored me and helped me grow as a Christian, a leader, and a speaker. And finally, he pushed me to become an author. This book would not have been possible without his encouragement, keen eye, and love to see this generation mobilized.

To the saints of Hinson Baptist Church, I thank you for welcoming us with open arms in the middle of a pandemic. You have shown my family what a healthy local church looks like. You've encouraged us and pointed us to the word and to worshiping the Lord.

ACKNOWLEDGMENTS

I wish to thank a number of friends who helped along the way. Justin Schell, a faithful mentor, pushed me to stay compassionate toward this generation. Andy Cimbala helped me to process our secular age. Neal and Whitney Woollard pushed me to publish.

I'm grateful for my mom and dad. I grew up in a home that loved Jesus and pushed me to love him as well. Through their life-long witness, I've seen an example of faithful endurance through trials and suffering. Through all the stages of my life, they've been there to support and push me to take the next step.

Finally, I'm thankful for my wonderful wife, Amber. She believed in this book before I did. In fact, she told everyone I was writing a book about Gen Z before I could even put pen to paper. Amber has sacrificed her time to see this book come to life. She has been a sounding board for ideas and stories. These past five years of marriage have flown by—may the Lord continue to give us many years to come! I love you and I like you.

I

Misunderstood

YEET. Do you know the meaning of this word? Could you use it in a sentence? Have you never heard of "yeet" before? Well, that may be a problem. Not because the word "yeet" will change your life, but because if you have never heard of this word, you have most likely missed much more about today's young and promising generation: Gen Z.

Recently, I was talking with some friends about Generation Z. They have younger kids and wondered if their kids were members of Gen Z. If they were born between the years of 1995 and 2012, the answer is yes.[1] People born between 1980 and 1995 are Millennials and people born after 2012 are what will, potentially, be called the Alpha Generation. My friends' kids were on the youngest end of Gen Z. As we began to talk about Gen Z, I shared some lingo their kids were bound to know, and one of those words was "yeet."

Our friends laughed and said, "Yeet? There is no way our kids know what 'yeet' is."

To which I replied, "Wanna bet? I bet they do!"

So, we called the kids into the living room, and I asked them if they knew the word "yeet." To my delight and to the chagrin of my friends, the kids, all of them, began to chant "Yeet! Yeet!

1. Twenge, *iGen*, 6.

YEET!" The chanting continued. The chanting turned to dancing. The dancing furthered the bewilderment of their parents.

They said, "So, you *do* know the word 'yeet'?"

One of the kids responded, "Know it? It's my favorite word!" Mouths gaping. "In fact, dad, it's my username for online gaming! My username is YeetNugget."

YeetNugget.

Though not every member of Generation Z will regularly use yeet, they've all heard it. If this vocabulary word is new to you, there is a lot more to come. Fortunately, you are not alone; you are in the same situation as many. We all learned a valuable lesson that night: *we don't know what we don't know.*

What if you, the reader, don't know what you don't know? What if you have missed something about Generation Z? What if you are missing out on the slang, the stories, the worldview, the motivations, and the big decisions? When dealing with the lives of the next generation, there is more on the line than misunderstanding the word "yeet."

From that night on, my friends took a step back and asked what else they were missing. What were they missing about the world of their kids? What did they misunderstand about the rules they lived by? We should do the same.

My journey with Generation Z started a few years ago. When I graduated from college, I began to work with a ministry called The Traveling Team. For six years I traveled campus to campus, working with university students. I served as a guest speaker at campus ministries on over three hundred campuses around the US. My role was to teach the story of Scripture from Genesis to Revelation and inspire the next generation to care about God's heart for all nations.

It was not until three years into my work that I began to notice many of the university students I was interacting with were different from me. These differences were not easy to spot at first, but as I began to study more on Generation Z, it finally registered that I was a younger Millennial, and I was interacting with members of

Gen Z. Millennials and those in Gen Z are not the same. They are different!

The members of Gen Z seemed to have a different worldview and value system than the worldview and value system I lived by. It was like crossing cultures. Their words were not my words, and their jokes did not make me laugh! As I compared their value system with the value system of older Millennials, Gen Xers, and Baby Boomers, I noticed there were large differences between the ministries serving these students and the students themselves. Just like parents, many campus ministers and pastors don't know what they don't know.

Generation Z is different from the Millennial generation and any previous generation. Let me be clear: differences are not bad. And also, differences should not be surprising. Each and every generation is different from another. However, these differences leave room for misunderstanding, mistreatment, and underrating this promising group of young people. They may seem like misfits, but let me tell you: those in Gen Z are promising and passionate. From firsthand experience, when Gen Zers have a heart changed by the gospel of Jesus Christ, they are a force that dreams bigger and more creatively than you can imagine. Gen Z is a generation of misfits and dreamers.

If you are picking up this book, it is likely you are in some way, shape, or form connected with Gen Z. That means you could be a member of Gen Z yourself or a member of an older generation who connects regularly with Gen Z. Whether you are eighteen, thirty-eight, or eighty-eight, my encouragement is to let this book spark your curiosity and compassion. Let the topics covered, in brief, ignite your interest in full. Let your new understanding drive you to care for and empower Gen Z.

THE GAP

If you were to get on a subway in London, or, as they call it, the tube, you would hear a constant announcement of "mind the gap." It's a warning to pay attention to the distance between where you are standing and the entryway onto the subway. In order to get on the subway safely, you need to take a big enough step. If you don't mind the gap, the consequences are catastrophic.

A gap is the distance between where you are and where you want to be. In relationships, a gap is the distance between where you are and where someone else is. Understanding this distance helps you better engage with them.

Such is the reality of the gap between older generations and younger ones. There is a gap between older generations and Gen Z: A gap when it comes to upbringing, worldview, and historic events. A gap in understanding life's problems, motivations, and the big decisions. A gap when thinking about religion, the Bible, Jesus, and the gospel. This gap leaves room for misunderstanding and catastrophe.

A misunderstanding of Gen Z is a large misunderstanding. Why? Because Gen Z makes up over seventy million people in the US—close to 20 percent of the population.[2] This means Gen Z is the largest generation currently living in the US. Its members are the young people of today, meaning they will be the leaders of tomorrow. We should care about Gen Z because we are parents or grandparents to members of Gen Z. We are coworkers with Gen Zers. We are looking to hire members of Gen Z. We are classmates and friends with members of Gen Z. Some of you reading this are members of Gen Z! Let God's heart for this generation of misfits and dreamers become your heart for this generation.

The purpose of this book is to bridge the gap between older generations and the seventy million members of Gen Z. I want to change the narrative on how older generations understand Gen Z. God, the maker of heaven and earth, desires to see those in Gen Z come to know him and desires for them to make him known. In order to change this narrative, we must first understand the world of Gen Z and what motivates members of this generation. We need to understand the gap between our world and their world— growing up then and growing up now. Then, through the application of biblical truth, we will explore how the Lord desires older

2. Twenge, *iGen*, 10.

generations to compassionately engage Gen Z. We will conclude with the trans-generational gospel of Jesus Christ and how the Christian life is a call to countercultural living. The greatest need of Gen Z is to hear and respond to the gospel; let us not forget it.

This book is not to be an exhaustive commentary on Gen Z, but a primer. A primer is an introduction to a topic. For those of us who don't know what we don't know, let's spend some time learning about the world members of Generation Z inhabit and the motivations driving them. We need to fill in the knowledge gap before we reflect on what it means for older generations to engage with Gen Z.

Many books on generations will jump straight to data and then solutions for a generation. The problem is, they often misinterpret the story of the generation. We don't need to know simply *how* a generation is different, but *why* a generation is different. As Christians, we need to learn to think well about members of Gen Z in order to better love them. Maybe you see them as misfits, but Jesus loved the misfits. We need to understand their story and what it means to invite them into a better story. Older Christians must bridge the gap between them and Gen Z!

The purpose of this book is not to provide the blueprint on how to reach Gen Z. It will not contain short steps to grow your ministry. It will not provide the three questions to ask to see members of Gen Z follow Jesus. The book will not solve all of your parenting issues. This book will, however, start you on the path of the hard work of engaging with this generation of misfits and dreamers.

CHANGING THE NARRATIVE

Recently, my younger brother, a member of Gen Z, informed me that I must dislike Gen Z because I've done so much study on them! To tell the truth, the narrative surrounding generations is negative. There is little praise and compassion for contrasting generations. The older generations undervalue the younger, and the younger generations dishonor the older generations. On top of that, as we explore the world of Gen Z, we will see that the narrative the world offers people in this generation is not the narrative the Lord would want them to follow. How do we change the narrative on generations?

The best way to confront this negative narrative is to truly understand the story of Gen Z. When there is a gap between older and younger generations, it is easier to stay uninformed and to make assumptions about the other group. As Christians, we should lovingly span the gap by seeking to understand differences and the impact they make on relationships. We don't just need data and next steps; we need compassion and a better narrative to share with them.

I want to balance celebrating the extraordinary qualities of this generation while taking a hard look at the obstacles and hurdles Gen Zers face as a generation. I desire to celebrate the image of God in each person, while also recognizing everyone, every generation, is sinful and broken. Every single person in every single generation needs the grace that comes through repentance and faith in Jesus Christ alone. Every single person in every generation must seek to align their heart and values to the God who created them. The narrative behind age and generations in Western culture is divisive, but God invites us to love and care for each generation because he cares about them.

God invites us to change that negative narrative and invite Gen Z to live a countercultural narrative. Psalm 78 is a rich psalm speaking about generations. Specifically, it focuses on recounting the history of Israel so people may look to the faithfulness of God and the unfaithfulness of his people.

In Psalm 78 the writer says,

> "He established a testimony in Jacob and appointed a law in Israel, which he commanded our fathers to teach to their children, *that the next generation might know them,* the children yet unborn, and arise and tell them to their children so that they should set their hope in God and not forget the works of God, but keep his commandments . . ." (emphasis added).

In this psalm, the author, Asaph, reminds God's people of the faithful acts God has done throughout Israel's history and how these stories of God's faithfulness should be the stories they tell their children. For Israel, looking back at how the Lord has worked in the past should be inspiration for the future.

This psalm is instructive for us on two fronts as we think about changing the narrative on Gen Z. First, Psalm 78 teaches us that the Lord cares for all generations. He does not just care for one generation or another. He cares for this generation and the next. This is obvious, but it seems to be so often overlooked. Second, Psalm 78 teaches us that the responsibility of the older generations is to tell the younger generations of God's faithfulness. Older generations counteract the narrative of the world by sharing the narrative of God's work throughout history.

Throughout the story of Scripture, the Lord cares for all people. He cares for the old and the young, the slave and the free, the Jew and the gentile, the believer and the nonbeliever. Is it possible that older generations have not taken enough interest in the younger? Is it possible that the issue of young people walking away from God has something to do with the lack of intentionality, care, and compassion of older generations? I think so.

The Lord's instruction for impacting the next generation is to recount his praiseworthy acts. The solution to reaching those in Gen Z is not the next short-term fad in the parenting or ministry world. It would be easy for me to tell you to get the next big social media platform and influence them that way. But then my advice would change tomorrow. We should not build our solutions on ever-moving targets!

LOOKING FORWARD

The way forward for engagement with members of Gen Z is twofold. First, we mind the gap. Second, we recount the Lord's praiseworthy acts throughout history and thereby invite members of Gen Z to reorient their stories with God's story. In other words, we *understand* the narrative, and we *change* the narrative. We don't invite them to align with our personal narrative for their lives, we invite them to align their lives with God and his purposes for all people. Yes, it takes the work of the Holy Spirit in someone's heart to want to follow God's ways, but as Christians we must be faithful witnesses to all people.

We will follow this twofold approach throughout the book. We will examine the world of Gen Z and the gap between Gen Z and other generations. We'll see how the world impacts Gen Zers' motivations. We'll think about the motivations that older generations should have toward Gen Z. We'll recount the story of Scripture from Genesis to Revelation and what it means for Gen Z today. Additionally, each chapter will have reflection questions to help span the gap between older generations and Gen Z. These will be key to the process of engaging with this next promising generation.

Before we get too ahead of ourselves, we need to be introduced to the world and motivations of Gen Z. We may understand that God cares for everyone in Gen Z, but we misunderstand who they are. We don't know what we don't know about this generation of misfits and dreamers. Let's span the gap by going back to the basics.

Yeet.

REFLECTION: BRIDGING THE GAP

1. Ask yourself what do you think are common characteristics and shared experiences among members of Gen Z? Make a list.

2. Ask Gen Zers what they think common characteristics and shared experiences are for their generation.

3. Compare your list with their list. What are the similarities and differences?

2

Our Changing World

THE YEAR 1995 WAS a big year. In 1995 Michael Jordan came out of retirement to lead the Chicago Bulls to three more NBA championships. In 1995, the Dallas Cowboys won the Super Bowl; it was the third win in four years—the first team in history to accomplish this. In 1995 personal computers began to enter homes at a faster rate, while the internet got its start. In 1995 Pluto was the furthest planet from earth in the solar system. In 1995 Bill Clinton was President, and he confirmed that Area 51 existed. In 1995 Starbucks began to serve a drink called the Frappuccino and had 667 stores around the world.

In 1995 the first members of Generation Z were born. Gen Zers would continue to be born until 2012.

By 2012 the world was a different place. LeBron James, who was eleven years old when Jordan came out of retirement, was an NBA MVP and the next basketball superstar. By 2012 computers and the internet ruled the world. By 2012 Pluto was no longer considered a planet in the solar system. By 2012 Starbucks offered free Wi-Fi to all customers at their eighteen thousand stores worldwide. By 2012 Bieber fever had struck the world, and the hearts of teenage girls are still recovering.

The biggest notable change in the world by 2012 was the smartphone: a supercomputer connected to the internet in your pocket at all times. By 2012, Apple released the iPhone 5 and social media and the online entertainment economy were in full swing. By 2012 the top smartphone apps included: Facebook (started in 2005), YouTube (started in 2005), Twitter (started in 2006), Netflix (started online streaming in 2007), Instagram (started in 2010), and the game *Angry Birds*.

The year 2012 marked the final birth year in Generation Z. The question we must ask is, what is Generation Z like? How big of a gap is there between Gen Z and other generations? How are Gen Zers different, and why should we care? What makes them tick? What formed them into the people they are? What is forming them into the people they will become?

It is not possible to cover every aspect of Gen Z. I want us to learn the basics of Generation Z: the core aspects of the world that shaped the people in Gen Z and the motivations driving them. I want to help you think biblically and compassionately about this promising generation. The call to live a Christlike life is not a call for only those in Generation Z; it is a call for anyone who follows Jesus from the ages of nine to ninety-nine!

WHY "GENERATION Z"?

So, what does "Generation Z" even mean? Why Z? Simply put, before Millennials were named Millennials, they were called Generation Y. And Generation Y was named Generation Y because the generation before them was called Generation X. So those born between 1995 and 2012 inherited the next letter of the alphabet. Hello Generation Z!

As of now, Generation Z has not been named anything other than Generation Z. There have been many advocates for other names such as iGen, Pivotals, The Founders, Plurals, Deltas, or Internet Generation—but none of these have stuck. It seems that Generation Z is keeping its name because its members haven't made a major move on desiring to change it. For the purposes of this book, we will stick to Generation Z—or Gen Z. Before we study who they are, let's understand the term "generation."

WHAT IS A GENERATION?

Each generation is a product of its time and place. The term generation means "a group of individuals born and living contemporaneously."[1] Three aspects shape each generation: birth years, defining moments, and societal trends. We'll start with birth years.

Birth years are key to understand when we think of generations because it's what distinguishes one generation from another chronologically. Baby Boomers were born between 1946 and 1964. Gen Xers were born between 1964 and 1980. Millennials were born between 1980 and 1995. Gen Zers were born between 1995 and 2012. However, birth years are not the only ingredient.

Understanding a generation is a complex matter. Too quickly do we jump to the characteristics, values, and personalities of individuals within a generation before looking at trends that have influenced them. Too quickly do we evaluate the whole by looking at a small sample. Too quickly do we assume a generation stands alone, without first understanding how the world, and previous generations, have influenced it.

The problem with only using the dictionary definition above is it misses the impact of the world in which those individuals are born and living. What shapes the members of a generation is more than the date they were born. It is also the era in which they were born. An era is a distinct period of time with specific characteristics. We understand this idea instinctually. We know life in the nineteenth century was different from life in the twentieth century. And we understand that the 1980s were different from today. Thus, being born at different times means people will have different experiences and different values as a result of those experiences.

What makes Gen Zers, Gen Zers is that they have a common experience, upbringing, and worldview—just as what makes Boomers, Boomers is the fact they too have a common experience, upbringing, and worldview. Each generation collectively experiences a few era-shaping events. I like to call these "defining

1. "Generation," definition b.

moments." We know World War II affected people of that time, and the smartphone affects people of this time. But defining moments have impacted this era, this generation.

I remember the day perfectly. I was in third grade and the best thing ever happened: the intercom in my classroom came on and requested that I come to the office. My parents were checking me out of school for the day. Bingo! There may be no better feeling to a kid in school.

I remember going home with my mom and asking her why I got checked out of class. She tried to describe to me, a third grader, what was happening. The date was September 11, 2001. Two planes had just hit the Twin Towers in New York City. At this point, nobody knew who it was or why it was happening, but it did not seem like an accident. As more information came out after these accidents—turned attacks—I still struggled to understand the meaning behind them. I will never forget that day and how those events shaped the world around me.

Each generation has defining moments that impact those in it. These defining moments shape their values. For *Millennials*, a defining moment is 9/11. You could scarcely meet a member of the Millennial generation who could not recall where they were when 9/11 happened. There are other defining moments for Millennials such as Barack Obama becoming the first black President of the United States, gay marriage being legalized in the US, and the introduction of the smartphone.

The same is true for other generations. For *Boomers*, the Vietnam War, the death of J.F.K., and the space race are defining moments. For *Gen Xers*, those defining moments would be events like the Watergate scandal and the AIDS epidemic.

For Gen Zers, a defining childhood moment was the Great Recession in 2008–2009 where the housing market crashed. It was in this recession that Gen Zers saw parents and relatives lose houses, cars, businesses, and jobs—their very livelihood uprooted. Losses like these led to strained and broken relationships in the home as well. For a child at home, they saw and sensed the fear of this time. Just like I didn't fully comprehend the impact of 9/11, I know that it changed the world around me. The same is true for Gen Z and the Great Recession. The Great Recession scarred Generation Z.

Similar to the Great Recession, the COVID-19 pandemic was a defining moment for this generation. From the uncertainty of the economy to the fear of sickness, to online school, the pandemic made a huge impact. Yes, everyone alive today was impacted by the pandemic, but can you imagine having your senior year of high school and graduation canceled because of a virus? Can you imagine missing the first year or two of junior high school because of a virus? The pandemic made its mark on Gen Z.

Other defining moments for Gen Zers would include the rise of social media, shootings in schools, Donald Trump becoming president, and the increase of racial tension in the US. The list could go on and on. Each moment may not have the same impact on each individual in the generation, because of different birth years, but they have shaped the generation as whole. We'll explore many of these moments in the chapters following.

It can be easy for us to look at the news and think things happening in the world simply transpire and don't transform the world. However, these defining moments shape and transform the world and each generation alive. Defining moments impact us!

Every single time I go to the airport, I must arrive early, stand in a long line, take off my shoes, belt, and jacket, empty my water bottle, and open my backpack and remove my computer. I then have to stand in line, go through some type of scanning machine, and then answer questions about the contents of my bags. In today's world, this is the new normal. This was not normal before 9/11.

Events can change the world around us, and in turn these moments shape our values. But defining moments are only part of the picture of generations. Cultural and societal trends shape generations as well.

The third impactful aspect in understanding generations is changing societal trends. Culture norms change. Many aspects of society change, like religion, politics, economics, family life, fashion, entertainment, and technology. This section is not a commentary on what societal changes have taken place but is meant to help us see how societal changes are helpful in understanding generations.

When examining a specific generation, we need to understand that each generation builds on the foundation laid by previous generations. Generations tend to correct and respond to aspects of the past. Those in each generation are shaped by the past, but they have their eyes on the future. Gen Zers are building their identity from pieces of the past.

For example, when we think about sexuality in society today, there appears to be a general trend away from the biblical norm. Many would trace this general trend back to the Sexual Revolution of the 1960s. So, it is true Gen Zers are continuing the societal trend by redefining sexuality, gender, and relationship norms, but they are not the ones who started the trend. Previous generations like Gen X and the Boomers helped to build the foundation.

To take a less serious topic, Gen Zers seem to approach social media differently from the way Millennials do. In the early 2000s there was a norm for how one conducted oneself online, but that norm is changing. Millennials were the first generation to fully adopt social media. There are advantages and disadvantages to this. One disadvantage is that Millennials seemed to overshare their lives on social media, to the detriment of their friends, family, and jobs. When someone gets fired for what they post, it's probably a Millennial! Gen Zers grew up seeing that there was too much oversharing on the internet, and they have now shifted their social media usage to platforms that favor privacy over constant public sharing.

There is a clear pattern to societal change among generations. The people in each generation will do one of two things. Either they will follow the trends of generations before them, or they will define themselves against those trends. They will either let the trends of the past define them, or they will seek to change the trends for the future.

To recap, this is what shapes those in a generation: *the years they were born, the defining moments, and societal trends.* From these core areas we can better understand Gen Z.

GEN Z'S MOTIVATIONS

In a typical book on generations, the authors may take you through some material similar to what we just looked at, by exploring the birth years of the generation and then how certain moments in history have impacted those people. Typically, this is where information on the context of the generation stops. Many tend to draw a straight line from these simple observations to actions and behaviors of Gen Zers.

I believe this cuts out a huge part of the story! Those in Gen Z are not simply a conglomeration of all their behaviors existing alone in a vacuum. They have motivations, and those motivations stem from the world they grew up in. My hope is to share this context so that we may think well about Gen Zers. I want to summarize their core motivations in four simple words so we may better understand the relationship between the world they grew up in and motivations they hold.

So, what motivates members of Gen Z?

- Connection
- Caution
- Causes
- Customization

These four words will be expanded upon in chapter 6, but they should get our wheels turning as we explore the world of Gen Z over the next three chapters. We'll see how the motivations of Gen Zers are shaped by their world, but let me define each word for you here.

Connection: Gen Zers are more connected than any previous generation. Though people in this generation tend to spend less time in person with friends, they are deeply relational. Equipped with a smartphone and an internet connection, Gen Zers can talk to anyone, anywhere, anytime.

Caution: Gen Zers are pragmatic and risk averse. They see the world through the lens of risk and practicality, which affects the way they think about their identity, relationships, careers, and futures.

Causes: Gen Zers care about what is happening in the world. Step on the campus of any four-year university today, and you will find students championing causes. Through the internet and social media, they see many problems in the world, and they dream of a better world.

Customization: Gen Zers have more options than any previous generation. They can customize their online profiles, coffee orders, and favorite clothes. Over-choice is a real issue for Gen Z.

Don't Miss the Trees for the Forest

Before we dive deeper into the world that those in Generation Z live in and how this affects their values, let me offer a caution: don't miss the trees for the forest. What do I mean? Generations are made of individuals. Though I will be speaking in general about the forest, the generation as a whole, don't forget there are individual people who are members of this generation.

Do not use these four motivations to critique every member of Gen Z. Each individual in Gen Z may reflect these motivations to varying degrees. Just like a single citizen of a specific country is not the core representative for that country, so a single member of Gen Z does not represent the whole generation.

The reverse is also true. There seem to be characteristics that are generally true for Americans, or Bulgarians, or Chinese, or for Zimbabweans. However, each individual is not the same. There is diversity within the unity and unity within the diversity. The same is true for Gen Z: each individual is not the same.

Gen Z is diverse. Diverse in fashion, language, culture, interest, and convictions. Its members are misfits in the best sense of the word. There is, however, a thread that unifies much of the diversity in Gen Z: secularism. Secularism is a belief system that undergirds everything everyone does, but nobody talks about it. Let's turn to understanding what secularism means for you, me, and Gen Z.

REFLECTION: BRIDGING THE GAP

1. Ask yourself, what defining moments did you experience growing up? What societal trends did you inherit from previous generations?

2. Ask Gen Zers what defining moments in their childhoods have impacted their lives. What societal trends did they inherit from your generation?

3. Ask Gen Zers in what ways they think they are similar to or different from other members of their generation.

3

Our Secular World

RECENTLY, I WENT ON a journey to find water. I had purchased a watercooler base but could not find any shop selling the five-gallon water jugs. This was a shockingly difficult task. Everywhere I looked, I came up dry. When I thought all hope was lost, I made one final search on Google and a store popped up called The Water Brewery. It piqued my interest. I love brewed things like coffee, tea, and kombucha—but I couldn't figure out what "brewing water" meant. I had no other options, so I took my chances and drove to the store.

When I arrived, The Water Brewery was a small, quaint shop. As I entered, I found everything I had been looking for—and more. The place was filled with water jugs and water dispensers. I had found an oasis in the desert.

I met the owner, a jovial man named Sam. He could not stop talking about how they sold the best water in town. Their water had special qualities. Sam said he filtered the water multiple times, treated it with UV light, enhanced it with electrolytes, and then spiritually charged it to rid it of negative energy and emotion. Wait, what? Yes, he said the water was spiritually charged to remove *emotion* from the water. This is what brewing water meant.

Sam spoke about the water as if it was a spiritual experience to taste it. He said tasting the water would enhance the god within us, which naturally led to further questions.

I asked Sam what enhancing god within us meant to him. I then asked Sam what he thought about God and if he had any specific thoughts about Jesus. Surprisingly, Sam loved talking about Jesus. He said he loved many of Jesus' sayings in the book of Matthew. He expressed sadness, saying Christians had misunderstood Jesus, thinking him to be higher and more godlike than an average human. Sam shared that Christians have twisted the words of Jesus, and they do not truly understand his nature and purpose. He told me he had a hard time believing what the Bible says about Jesus because it did not jibe with what he thought of the world. He said he watched many videos, and they confirmed his suspicions.

When I asked more about Jesus' true nature and purpose, Sam leaned in and whispered to me, "Well, most people don't know this, but Jesus didn't ascend to heaven."

"Oh, really?" I said inquisitively.

"Yes. Jesus did not ascend to heaven. Jesus ascended to the New Jerusalem."

"Where's that?" I asked, thinking he didn't sound too crazy.

"Well, the New Jerusalem is actually a gigantic spaceship orbiting Saturn. One day, the New Jerusalem Spaceship will land on earth when mankind is truly ready to receive the message Jesus intended to share."

Conversations at the watercooler are always interesting, but this one spun me for a loop.

Over the last several decades, the average person's conclusions about God, the Bible, and truth have changed in the West. Sam is post-Christian and post-truth. These conclusions and this conversation are the fruits of our secular age.

WHAT IS SECULARISM?

I was born in Arkansas, which basically means I was born in church. It's the South: the Bible Belt. So, being born in a church, the term "secularism" did not mean too much to me. When I thought of someone being secular, I thought of someone being an atheist. My simple logic went like this: If I'm a Christian, then I'm not influenced by the secular.

I was wrong.

The rise in secularism is not a rise in a specific set of beliefs, like atheism or agnosticism; instead it is a change in the *conditions of belief*.[1] Before secularism changes specific beliefs, it changes the way we think about beliefs. The rise of secularism is a historical event. It is a shift in the world and in history—not in an individual.

I am influenced by secularism.

You are influenced by secularism.

Gen Z is influenced by secularism.

Being secular *can* mean someone is less religious, but religion is not the whole story. We can be tempted to think too simplistically about the story of secularism. Before we turn to see how secularism impacts Generation Z, we will explore the story of secularism and the core values it thrusts upon the world today.

Not the Story of Secularism

When I think about someone being secular, I think they are less religious. In fact, this is the story many atheists tell Christians about the world. It is what the great Catholic philosopher Charles Taylor calls "the subtraction story."[2]

The subtraction story goes like this: Over time, humanity has progressed and become more and more dependent on itself. As a result, humans have less and less need for any type of God. We've subtracted God from the equation of life. As a result of this, many people are leaving traditional faith. In fact, the subtraction story holds there will be a day when nobody believes in a God at all.

Have you heard this story before?

1. Taylor, *A Secular Age*, 3.
2. Taylor, *A Secular Age*, 26.

Taylor says this subtraction story it not the full story of secularism. The story is not quite so simple. Taylor wrote an eight-hundred-page book called *A Secular Age* to tell the more complicated story and the impact the story has on today's world. The rise of secularism is not a throwing off of old ideas but an invention of new ideas.[3]

In an abbreviated version, the story goes like this: Five hundred years ago it was nearly impossible to find someone who did not believe in God in the West. Today, belief is never taken for granted. Five hundred years ago, people lived in a world that saw God as real, external to humans, and able to impact their lives. Over the last several centuries, the world has been considered in more materialistic forms. Eventually, many came to see the world as wholly material, with no influence from a higher being, no creator. A god who cannot interact with the world and our lives is no god at all.

These news ideas about God led to the rise of the first clear alternative to the Christian faith in the West: *humanism*. Humanism considers human beings to be the starting point for determining morality and purpose. In humanism, humans are the center, rather than the divine God.[4] In humanism, people desire to have the benefits of God's kingdom without God as king.[5] In short, people no longer think of themselves in terms of their relationship with the Creator, but instead they think of themselves in terms of their material world.

If you take Taylor's story of secularism and overlay it with the world today, it will begin to make more sense. As humanism moved the focus from God to mankind, mankind became further fixated on the individual. Humanism gave way to individualism. The proof is in today's most popular sayings:

- You be you.
- Treat yourself.

3. Taylor, *A Secular Age*, 22.
4. Taylor, *A Secular Age*, 299.
5. Sayers, *Disappearing Church*, 79.

- Focus on self-love today.
- Be your best self.
- Follow your heart.[6]

Do these sayings sound familiar? If so, you are well acquainted with the most palpable fruit of secularism today: *expressive individualism.*

Expressive Individualism

Expressive individualism is the ideology driving people's thinking today. Culture in the West is fixated on self. The culture in which we live is obsessed with getting you to love you more. Individualism says you are independent. Who you are is not determined by a government, a church, or a group of people, it is determined by yourself.

The culture of expressive individualism encourages people to be their own person, find their own way, and ultimately find fulfillment in self-discovery.[7] In a culture of expressive individualism, we *express our individuality* through clothing, social media, sexuality, brand identity, political party, and whatever else signals to the world around us our expression of self. The only sin in this paradigm is hindering others from finding their true selves or from expressing their true selves.

Let me be clear: individuals are important. You are important. God, in his sovereignty, works through individuals. In Exodus, God works through Moses to lead the people of Israel out of captivity. In II Samuel, God establishes a covenant with David, an individual, that would impact the world. Jesus, God incarnate, lives and dies and rises again to redeem all who turn and trust in him. The Lord works through individuals!

But you are not the most important person in the universe. The secular ideal of the expressive individualism is thoroughly

6. Wax, "Expressive Individualism."
7. Taylor, *A Secular Age*, 299.

unbiblical. God, the maker of the heavens and earth, should be the center of our life, work, devotion, and worship. Not ourselves. Humans have always struggled with idolatry, or self-worship. Let's look at the impact of expressive individualism and secularism on the world of Gen Z.

SECULARISM IN OUR SOCIETY

The world we live in impacts the values we hold. The same is true for Gen Z and secularism. Everyone has been impacted by secularism. I will argue that Generation Z's values are only different from previous generations' values because the worldview of secularism has further taken hold of the world we all live in. As the world grows more secular, so too does each successive generation.

Secularism has impacted the world of Generation Z in three core areas: religion, truth, and sexuality. The landscape of these three areas has shifted due to the ever-increasing rise of expressive individualism.

Religion

I recently met an international student from Germany who was studying in Indiana. This international student was attending Bible studies and events through a local church and enjoyed discussing spiritual topics. When I asked her about her upbringing, she said she had zero religious upbringing. The student told me she had only been in a church one or two times and had no frame of reference to understand Jesus, church, the Bible, or anything she was learning. The student said she does not know a single religious person at home, so if she wanted to continue her spiritual journey, she would not even know how. She is from the country where the Protestant Reformation took place five hundred years ago. The conditions of belief have changed in Europe.

Europe is ahead of the United States in departure from religious activity, but this problem is not a problem for "those people over there," it is a problem for us here and now. I was at the skate park once, and I met a teenager who told me he was Catholic. As I asked about his spiritual background, he told me his entire family was Catholic, and they only went to church on Christmas and Easter. I asked him what he knew about Jesus and why Jesus came to earth. The teenager gave me a blank stare. He told me he didn't know enough to even begin to tell me who Jesus was. He was Catholic but did not know a thing about what Catholics believe. The conditions of belief have changed in the United States. The West is less religious now than it was fifty years ago, and less religious fifty years ago than it was one hundred years ago.

Jean Twenge, an expert on Gen Z, says Generation Z is the least religious generation in US history. She observed that 94 percent of college freshman in 1966 were affiliated with religion, but in 2016 the number was 69 percent.[8] This is a continued trend from culture, not something Gen Z started. The world is becoming less and less religious, generation by generation.

Many have called this phenomenon among younger generations "the rise of the nones." The word *none* is used to describe what younger generations answer on religious surveys. When asked about their religious affiliation, they do not answer Christian, Muslim, or atheist, they answer *none*. Many in the younger generation see themselves with zero religious upbringing and zero religious affiliation.[9]

There is much to be said about the rise of the nones. Author and Pastor James Emery White describes the rise of the nones as a change in the "squishy center." He says over the last couple of hundred years there has always been a "squishy center" caught between strong religious polarities.[10] There have been people adamantly for religion and people adamantly against religion, and there have always been people caught in the middle (squishy center) who just

8. Twenge, *iGen*, 128.

9. White, *Meet Generation Z*, 20.

10. White, *Meet Generation Z*, 30.

went with the majority culture belief. Today, the majority culture trends toward nonbelief, apathy, and self-love. Since the majority culture trends toward unbelief, the squishy center follows the majority.

The rise of the nones is real. As I have traveled to hundreds of university campuses across the US, I have seen a decline in overall religious activity. But there is hope! Though the "squishy center" has moved toward apathy, there are many young people today who have a passionate heart for God and are ready to impact the world. Don't count out Gen Z. The Christians among Gen Z are misfits, but they dream of making an impact on their generation and in the world.

Truth

With the shift in the religious landscape of today, there has been a shift in the understanding of truth. Due to expressive individualism, the ultimate authority of truth has shifted from someone external (God) to something internal (self). Both truth and authority are seen as solely internal.

Recently, I was at Montana State University speaking at a campus ministry on God's heart to reach the nations with the message of Jesus. Closing out the talk, I challenged the Christian college students to align their lives with this mission and to consider ways they could impact the nations. I communicated to the audience that the Great Commission is a command, an invitation to live differently from the world around us. The story of Scripture demands a response to the believer and the unbeliever. I poured my all into the message.

After the meeting, I was talking with a student. He said "Man, great talk. That's really good for you. I'm glad you found what God has called you do." Then he walked away.

What?

I had spent forty minutes laying out a biblical foundation on how all Christians should align their lives and purpose with what God is doing around the world. And his response was to tell me my message was a great message for me. Did he think I was up there talking to myself?

This is what a changing landscape of truth and authority looks like. Though not every person, or Christian, I interact with responds to Scripture and truth statements this way, it is becoming the new normal. This is a fruit of expressive individualism in the lives of Christians who make up Gen Z. In a world where you're told all truth and authority is found within yourself, it can be hard to listen to any other voice. The ultimate and final authority does not come from your parents, grandparents, pastor, boss, or friends, it comes from your personal feelings.

The shift in truth and authority is not a problem within the Christian world alone; it impacts all the members of Gen Z. A recent survey found only 4 percent of teens (ages thirteen to eighteen) have a biblical world view. The survey also reported only 34 percent believe lying is wrong.[11]

Barna, the group responsible for the survey says a biblical worldview consists of eight key factors:

1. Has made a personal commitment to Jesus that is still important in their life today

2. Believes they will go to heaven when they die "because you have confessed your sins and accepted Jesus Christ as your savior"

3. Strongly agrees the Bible is totally accurate in all of its teachings

4. Strongly agrees they personally have a responsibility to tell other people your religious beliefs

5. Strongly disagrees that Jesus Christ committed sins when he lived on earth

6. Strongly disagrees that the devil, or Satan, is not a living being but a symbol of evil

11. *Gen Z: The Culture*, 40.

7. Strongly disagrees that a person can earn a place in heaven if they are generally good or they do enough good things for others

8. Believes God is the all-powerful, all-knowing, perfect creator of the universe who rules the world today[12]

Only 4 percent of Gen Z agrees with the above definition!

When I was speaking in the Washington, DC, area, I met a campus staff who shared with me about the evangelism efforts of their ministry. The staff said the topic of sin had become more and more difficult to talk about, not because of fear, but because most of the students felt they had never actually done anything wrong. There was no sense of guilt in their lives.

The conversation changed when he began to talk about shame. The students understood this. The Gen Z students he was interacting with did not have a sense of guilt over sins, but they had a deep sense of shame. They did not feel they had done bad things. They felt they *were* bad. This is a massive shift in the psyche of this generation. Because of relative truth and authority, there is no right and wrong, only feeling. The good news is shame is a true and biblical reality of sin. The Bible says we are bad people who have done bad things. We need a good God to save us.

Though the landscape of truth has changed, the gospel is still good news. Guilt before a holy God must be addressed, but maybe starting a gospel conversation with shame would be more fruitful on the front end. Begin with shame and then move to guilt.

The world Generation Z lives in is post-Christian and post-truth, but expressive individualism has one final impact on the world of Generation Z today. Not only has secularism upended the world when it comes to religion and truth, but also when it comes to our understanding of sexuality and gender.

---

12. *Gen Z: The Culture*, 113.

Sexuality and Gender

Recently, I was speaking at a school in North Carolina. Typically, at the meeting there is a main group session and then the group breaks into men and women. This specific meeting offered a unique challenge, though. There was a male student I was trying to get into the guys group, when a campus minister told me this student may look male, dress male, and speak male, but he identifies as a female. Situations like these are now the normal on university campuses and even in Christian ministries. These issues are not distant, they are near. Sexuality and gender identity are the last major areas of impact secularism and expressive individualism have on the world of Gen Z. We live in a world with constantly changing definitions of sex, sexual orientation, and gender.

What seemed to begin in the 1960s in the sexual revolution actually had its foundations in secularism. Over the past fifty years there were major changes in marriage and sex on a cultural level. Over the past twenty-five years there were major changes in a cultural understanding of sexuality beyond heterosexuality. In the past ten years there have been major changes in a cultural understanding of gender. The rise of secularism and expressive individualism allows us to understand these trends.

The initials "LGBTQ" are a clear fruit of the changing views of sexuality. LGBTQ stands for lesbian, gay, bisexual, transgender, and queer. A simple look at the news or a college campus will illustrate the force of this movement and the rainbow flag so closely accompanying the letters.

Sexuality is an important topic for many members of Gen Z. It's a cause many in the generation are eager to support and participate in. In 2018, surveys reported one in eight members of Generation Z describe their sexual orientation as something other than heterosexual.[13] In 2011, a report by the *Washington Post* reported that one in six members of Generation Z are LGBTQ.[14]

---

13. *Gen Z: The Culture*, 40.
14. Schmidt, "1 in 6 Gen Z Adults Are LGBT."

The rise in changing sexual definitions is tied to moral and religious beliefs. One recent survey reported a decline in the belief that homosexual behavior is wrong. Only 20 percent of Gen Z believe homosexual behavior is morally wrong.[15]

The rise of secularism and the expressive individual are linked to the changing sexual identities of today. When the world tells you to seek your greatest pleasure, you try to find it. When the world tells you there is no truth, you determine right and wrong for yourself. When the world says you are the center of the universe, your values are shaped to revolve around you.

My wife and I live in Portland, Oregon. I'm not sure what comes to mind for you when you think of Portland, but odds are it's probably true. This city is a bastion of secularism and expressive individuality. The mantra of the city is "Keep Portland Weird." They are doing just that.

This is the city to people-watch. And don't get me started on Halloween.

Portland is one of America's most progressive, liberal, and secular cities. It is also a case study in a crumbling worldview. Portland is one of the least religious cities in the US, along with one of the most anxious and depressed cities.

Not long after moving to town, my wife and I were walking to dinner with a friend, and we happened upon a young lady who was crying, in the fetal position on the sidewalk. She was dressed nice and was obviously not homeless. She was just hurting.

We approached the young lady and sat next to her on the dirty city sidewalk. As we talked to her, she said her name was Steph, and all she could say was, "I'm not worthy. I'm not good enough. Why can't I be good enough? I just don't get it."

We asked some questions to understand exactly what she was talking about, and as she sobbed, she clarified: "I'm not worthy. I'm not good enough for him. Why can't I be good enough for him? I don't get what he needs."

We asked who "him" was, and she said it was her boyfriend. Her boyfriend wanted an open relationship, a relationship where

15. *Gen Z: The Culture*, 56.

they could date but also sleep with whoever else they wanted. She wanted him to be happy in his decision, but she couldn't handle the pressure personally. She told us she had multiple mental breakdowns and had attempted suicide.

The world was telling her: yes, yes, yes. You can be free. You can sleep with whoever you want. You can be what you want to be. However, all she wanted was a normal boyfriend.

Steph was twenty. Steph is a member of Generation Z. Her worldview was crumbling. She was filled with shame, she was anxious, but she had nowhere else to look for answers.

Secularism is not an idea, it is not a set of beliefs, it is not something we can wish away. It is here, and here to stay. It is embedded in the psyche of our world, and we are reaping the fruits of its ideas. Author and speaker James Smith says, "There's no undoing the secular; there is just the task of learning how (not) to live—and perhaps even believe—in a secular age."[16] We must all learn how to correctly believe in a secular age, including Gen Z.

Secularism is just part of the story and world Gen Z inhabits. If expressive individualism is Gen Z's moral compass, then technology and the internet is the tool used to execute the disastrous, self-fulfilling life. Let's look at how the phone in our pocket is shaping us more than anyone would have ever imagined.

REFLECTION: BRIDGING THE GAP

1. Ask yourself, how has the nature of secularism changed during your lifetime? What effects has it had on your understanding of faith or identity?

2. Ask Gen Zers what they think of secularism. Explain the idea of expressive individualism to them and ask how they have seen it impact their understanding of identity and purpose.

3. Ask Gen Zers (if age appropriate) in what ways they have seen identity tied to sexuality.

16. Smith, *How (Not) to Be Secular*, 11.

4

Our Connected World

IN 1995, A MOVIE came out that would change the world: *Toy Story*. This beloved animated movie is about a boy and his lively lost toys, a cowboy experiencing a midlife crisis, and an astronaut who thinks he can fly. The reason this movie changed the world was not because it changed the hearts and imaginations of all who watched, though it did. *Toy Story* changed the world because it was the first movie to ever be animated strictly using a computer.

The years 1995 and onward were booming years for personal computers and the internet. In fact, 1995 was the tipping point in internet usage. In 1995, Pew Research found that only 21 percent of people had ever used the internet. One year later it grew to 73 percent![1] It was known as the dot-com boom. In 1995, companies like eBay, Netscape, Amazon, Craigslist, and Yahoo started. People with internet connections began to crowd chat rooms, create an online economy, and share ideas on blogs.

The internet and personal computer growth would continue to grow until 2008 when Apple announced the iPhone. They promised to take the power of a home internet connection and put it in everyone's pocket.

What also took place between the rise of the internet and the smartphone? The majority of Gen Z was born. The growth of the

1. "Online Use in 1996."

internet correlates with the growth of a generation. Gen Z came of age in the internet age. Consider this: there is not a single member of Gen Z who can remember a world without the internet.

The internet, the computer, and the smartphone have all shaped Generation Z. These technologies have gripped not only Gen Z but older generations too! They have a unique transforming power on the minds of all. However, we must remember there is a difference between using a device when you are older and *being developed* by a device when you are younger. Gen Zers are digital natives. Any grandparent's computer problem is an everyday solution for teenagers.

When someone thinks of characteristics of Gen Zers, they often think of them as glued to their phones, engrossed in their messaging, or addicted to video games. People link today's technology with this generation. As we saw in the last chapter, secularism is the underlying value system of Gen Z. Technology is merely the tool Gen Zers use. To use another analogy, if the world of Gen Z were a building, secularism would be the foundation. Technology would be the walls.

Before we look at the specific technologies of the internet, social media, and the smartphone, let's make sure we understand what technology is and the role it plays in society.

TECHNOLOGY 101

A car is a fantastic piece of technology. Two hundred years ago people would have thought you were crazy if you told them you could drive a machine with four wheels anywhere you wanted. Today it's normal. And you do it while putting on mascara!

When is the last time you were amazed by the technology of the bicycle, or eyeglasses, or a bottle opener? Or toilet paper? Never! Yet these are all technology.

Technology is created by humans for our good. This understanding will help us as we seek to understand Gen Z's relationship with technology and how we can teach Gen Zers to master it instead of being mastered by it. A lesson we can all learn.

Tony Reinke in his book *12 Ways Your Phone Is Changing You* identifies nine realities tied to technology throughout human history.

1. Technology modifies creation

2. Technology pushes back the results of the fall

3. Technology establishes human power

4. Technology helps to edify souls

5. Technology upholds and empowers our bodies

6. Technology gives voice to human autonomy

7. God governs every human technology

8. Technology shapes every relationship

9. Technology shapes our theology[2]

Reinke does not make any specific mention of the internet, social media, or the smartphone in this list because technology is not merely today's reality; it is the reality of human existence. As the list shows, technology influences every area of human life: creation, sin, power, our souls, our bodies, relationships, and what we think of God.

Whether it be for the glory of God or the pride of man, technology is used in each generation. The good, the bad, and the ugly will come from technology. Technology can be wielded for great good or for great evil. Christians have used technology to share the word of God, whether that be by parchment, printed books, or the internet. In contrast, evil people, have used the latest technology available to push forward their agenda and wreak havoc on the world.

So, what technologies are uniquely impacting Gen Z? The internet, social media, and the smartphone are the culprits. Gen Zers cannot remember a day without an internet connection. They cannot fathom a social world that does not continue online. They

2. Reinke, *12 Ways*, 30–36.

cannot remember the last time they spent a few hours away from their smartphone. Maybe you can't either!

THE INTERNET: LIMITLESS CONTENT

The internet changed everything. Today, it's nearly impossible to function in society without an internet connection. Today the question is not "Do you have internet?" It is "What's the Wi-Fi password?"

Today we not only share ideas and connect with people on the internet, but we also stream movies, play video games, bank, work, listen to music, shop, plan vacations, navigate GPS, research restaurants, and order food. The internet has not only changed these activities, but it is also connecting everything together! Wi-Fi is placed everywhere: cars, washers and dryers, refrigerators, light bulbs, garage doors, security cameras, door locks, and more.

Google has taught us we can find *any answer* on the internet. Amazon has taught us we can *buy any item* from the internet. With the internet we are limitless. Every problem is solved by googling it. Before the internet, our knowledge was limited by our experience. Who did you know? What books did you read? Today, there is no limit. The internet is where we consume information, entertainment, and products.

For members of Gen Z, unlimited content has shaped their worldview. They are constantly being marketed to through the internet. They are asking the internet the answers to questions, both big and small. The internet has allowed them to follow whatever ideas they can dream up. For those who are not members of Gen Z, we can remember when we received unlimited access to all we could possibly imagine. Gen Z has always had this.

SOCIAL MEDIA: LIMITLESS CONNECTION

Connection and communication were core to the early days of the internet. There were blogs, chat rooms, and email chains. However, in the early 2000s, the internet found its first smashing success in connecting the general population: Facebook. In 2006, Facebook was opened to the public. It has remained the king since. Nearly 70 percent of Americans use Facebook.[3] There are over 2.9 billion monthly users around the world.[4] It's gone global.

People in Generation Z cannot remember a world without social media. For many, their parents used social media to document their sonograms, first steps, first day of school, first . . . everything. Naturally, social media has become the lifeblood of Generation Z. Let's not blame this generation for overuse of a product older generations created and connected them to.

Today, Facebook may have the most users, but it is not where Gen Z spends most of its time. The top apps used by this generation are Snapchat, Instagram, and TikTok. There are three primary differences between the way Gen Z uses social media and the way older generations use it.

First, Gen Zers tend to use social media privately. Where older generations may use more public social media platforms like Facebook and Twitter, Gen Zers opt for platforms where they can control what is public and what is private. Hence, the use of Snapchat, where everything disappears after 24 hours, or Instagram where you can tightly control who follows you and what they see.

Second, Gen Zers use social media to meet and engage with people they would otherwise never meet. Social media has made the world smaller. Gen Z is taking advantage of meeting like-minded people across the country and world. The internet has unified the world.

Third, Gen Zers curate their brand through social media. Where older generations may pick and choose certain things to post or delete from more public social media, much of the Gen Z users have a specific style, message, or brand connected with their account. Linked to this idea is the fact that many in Gen Z may have multiple user accounts on the same platform for different audiences. They may have one account that is more "raw" that

3. Perrin and Anderson, "U.S. Adults Using Social Media,"
4. "Number of Active Facebook Users."

only their friends see. Then they also have a more selective public profile for the rest of the world.

Social media is a necessity for members of Gen Z. Depending on who you ask, the effects of social media are positive or negative. One thing is certain: the smartphone has enabled social media to intersect every aspect of life.

THE SMARTPHONE

Today it is unheard of for a member of Gen Z to make it to high school without a smartphone. For Millennials, it was simply getting a cellphone. Today it's about getting the newest iPhone with unlimited data.

As access to smartphones increased, so has screen time. More than half of teens use screens more than four hours a day. One in four uses screens more than eight hours a day! Let that sink in. Eight hours a day. That seems insane. Not to them.[5]

Don't get me wrong. Before the smartphone, people did not just read books and exercise outside. Before the smartphone, there was still the laptop, the desktop computer, and the TV. But the smartphone is unique, because it combines everything we want in one handy device. The smartphone is the go-to device for Gen Z. The smartphone puts the power of unlimited content and connection into the pocket of anyone who has a few hundred dollars. However, it actually comes at a much higher cost.

THE EFFECTS: THE GOOD, THE BAD, AND THE UGLY

In junior high school I had one goal: to get home as fast as I could and hop on my computer. I was a gamer. I was hooked on a game called *World of Warcraft*. Over the course of three years, I logged over 150 days played. This means I played almost 3,600 hours in three years. I averaged playing three hours a day, every single day, for three years straight. That's commitment!

5. *Gen Z: The Culture*, 14.

Not only was I committed to the game, but I was also committed to my go-to beverage: Mountain Dew. And don't get me started on Hot Pockets. Did all of those hours have an effect on me? You bet.

Now, many would say 3,600 hours spent playing a single video game seems excessive. For me, these hours spent playing were not just a waste of time. To some extent, I benefited from playing this game. I learned skills like communication with other players, how to focus on a single task, how to problem solve, and how to manage money. Could I have learned these skills through some other platform? Yes. But I didn't. I learned them through *World of Warcraft*. I learned real life skills through a life-sucking game.

The effects of video games on my life are similar to the effects of the internet, social media, and the smartphone on Gen Z today. Are there benefits? Absolutely. But we all know unlimited consumption and unlimited connection without boundaries are a recipe for disaster. The internet, social media, and the smartphone can be used for many good things such as learning a new skill, connecting with friends, working remotely, or gaining a platform. But I don't need to remind you of the potential benefits of the devices you are using or addicted to. Instead, we must see the potential dangers in these technologies and how the power of unlimited content and connectivity are negatively impacting this promising generation.

The Bad: Limits in a Limitless World

Limits are an interesting thing. When was the last time you went to an all-you-can-eat buffet? I'm sure you did not leave feeling great about life. Our stomach thinks instead of our brain. We gorge ourselves and then realize it's too late.

We all have limits. As humans, we are created with limits, but we live in a world pushing us to the edge. Our hearts, eyes, and minds want more than we can handle. And the technologies of today promise we can have it all.

As adults, we should know better. Especially, as Christians. However, too often we trust our children to figure it out on their own. We have served Gen Zers an endless buffet of information, news, products, ideas, people, and then asked them to figure it out on their own. We have set them up for failure.

The bad about the internet, social media, and the smartphone is not the services or devices themselves. It is our fallen nature and broken hearts continually seeking to live past our limits and without God.

There are four major heart postures toward the tech of today that cause negative effects on Gen Z:

- Consumption without consideration
- Contribution without consequences
- Concern without control
- Connection without company

Consumption without consideration. The internet invites this generation to consume without considering the impact it has on their lives. Just like overconsumption at a buffet, so overconsumption on the internet has effects on the minds and hearts of people. We lack the wisdom to slow down and ask questions. We lack the ability to hit stop rather than play. Gen Z is overstimulated with videos and over saturated with new ideas. Many Gen Zers are unable to process everything that is happening. In fact, they are not even taught to consider the impact of all they consume.

Contribution without consequences. Social media invites its users to share their lives and stories for the world to see. It also invites you to share stories, ideas, and posts from other people you've never met. Blogs allow you to share your ideas without accountability. The comments section of a video allows you to comment without any consequence for your negative words. The anonymity of the internet leads to a lack of accountability. Without accountability, fake news, conspiracy theories, and someone else's story can be shared at rapid speeds before anyone has time to debunk or stop it.

A great example of this is a conspiracy theory that spread across on the internet in 2020. The conspiracy theory was that Wayfair, an online furniture retailer, was selling furniture with trafficked children inside.[6] The reasoning went like this: there was costly furniture that had names matching the names of children from the missing persons list. This story was shared, retweeted, and reposted thousands of times without readers stopping to consider the facts.

There are several problems with this story. First, why would a company seeking to traffic children name the furniture after the missing children? Not a great tactic. Second, did anyone search for similar furniture and find that it was priced at high prices at other retailers as well? Perhaps there is a reason that a cabinet cost $13,000. And finally, did anyone search to see if any of these missing children had been found? Across the internet, people were in uproar needlessly. The company was greatly impacted because of this conspiracy theory. We contribute to something without consequence. We consume a story without consideration.

Concern without control. The internet has allowed everyone, everywhere access to anything, anywhere. As a result, within minutes news on the other side of the world shows up as a notification on your phone. Gen Zers are rocked by events of the world no matter where they live. Constantly learning about a government uprising, or a natural disaster, or some other tragedy has negative effects. Gen Zers are concerned for many things happening in the world, though they have absolutely no control over them. Smartphones and the twenty-four-hour news cycle are a source of stress and anxiety for today's young people.

Connection without company. Social media promises that you can connect with anyone anywhere, but it is not a perfect substitution for authentic human interaction. It is a wonderful service that helps people connect with long-lost friends, relatives, and people from around the world, but it cannot be our only form of connection. Virtual meetings and video calls are not a one-for-one substitute for sharing a meal with a close friend. Only in the world

6. Golding, "Wayfair Product Listings."

of social media is it possible for someone to have a million followers or thousands of likes on a picture and yet feel completely lonely. Gen Z is left to figure out how to navigate relationships in a completely new world run by social media.

The Ugly: Consumption That Kills

If the bad side of these technologies is our lack of recognizing our limits, then the ugly side of the internet is doing things in *private* that we would never do in *public*. The ugly side of the internet is that we consume things that kill us without anyone else knowing.

The best example of this? Pornography.

Porn is deadly. It is accessible anywhere through a smartphone. It is also deemed acceptable by today's society. The average age of exposure to porn is twelve years old, and over 90 percent of teens and young adults are encouraging, accepting, or neutral on talking about porn with their friends.[7] Its ugliness is protected by the sexual ethic of our world. Our secular worldview turns sex and humans into something to be consumed rather than enjoyed. Something to use rather than someone with whom to connect.

There is no positive quality to pornography. Yet six in ten teens and young adults look at porn daily, weekly, or monthly.[8] Regular porn usage leads to the objectification of other people made in God's image, ruined marriages, broken relationships, and addicted brains. There are other aspects of the internet, social media, and smartphones that are ugly and evil, but pornography is the most prevalent, widely accessible, and damaging no matter the gender.

MOVING FORWARD

Older generations must help the younger. Have we given devices to our children, trusting them to do the responsible thing? They can't.

7. Covenant Eyes, "Porn Stats."
8. "Porn in the Digital Age."

The temptation is too great. How are we supposed to help Gen Z? What are we to do with the technologies of today? Are we to throw their phones and our phones in the trash? I hope not! Should we disconnect internet providers and go back to newspapers? I really hope not! But we can do two things to help Gen Z (and ourselves).

First, we need to help Gen Z grow in wisdom and discernment when it comes to our use of the internet, social media, and smartphones. Personally, what would it look like to use the features on many smartphones that tell you of your usage patterns? Then, what would it look like to discuss these usage patterns with your kids, your friends, or your spouse? What would it look like to create boundaries for when you can consume content and the type of content you consume? As older generations, we can lead out on wisdom and discernment in technology usage. Our example can help to lead Gen Z.

Second, we need to develop compassion to help Gen Z grow in wisdom and discernment with these technologies. Showing restraint in today's society is not applauded. The world is telling Gen Z to tap the link, purchase the product, and follow the influencer. We need to show we understand these difficulties and have nonjudgmental conversations with Gen Zers about these topics. It is key to recognize that everyone on social media and with a smartphone faces the same issues. How many times a day do you check your phone? How much screen time do you think you rack up? Should we remove the log from our eye before we take the speck out of Gen Z's? Yes, we should.

Surveys show only one in ten members of Gen Z are *digitally discerning*.[9] A digitally discerning teen is a teen who has low screen time and gives a lot of thought to the content they consume. Creating digitally discerning teens is crucial. Teens having a higher-than-average screen time are more likely to feel isolated, insecure, and critical of themselves. What would it look like for us to help Gen Z grow in digital discernment?

Gen Zers have a supercomputer in their pocket. They're not afraid to use it. In fact, they're afraid to stop using it. Secularism

9. *Gen Z Vol 2*, 7–8.

and the desire to be an expressive individual have pushed them to more use of these devices. They become anxious, depressed, and lonely. It is indeed a complex time to grow up—especially as the very definition of growing up changes with each generation.

REFLECTION: BRIDGING THE GAP

1. Ask yourself, how have the smartphone and social media changed your life in the last ten years?

2. Ask Gen Zers in what ways they have seen the smartphone and social media of today used for good.

3. Ask Gen Zers in what ways the smartphone and social media of today have caused harm.

5

Growing Up in Today's World

JOSH BASKINS WAS A NORMAL twelve-year-old in 1988. He had one problem. He was at a carnival, and he was too short to ride a specific ride. Then, also at this carnival, he found a fortune-telling machine that asked him to make a wish. He wished he were big.

The next day, Josh woke up . . . big. He had gone from a twelve-year-old boy to a full-grown man. His only friend did not believe him, and he could not tell his parents, but Josh was all grown up! Accepting that he was now grown, Josh tried to make his way by getting a job. At work, he found a love interest. Understandably, a twelve-year-old trapped in a man's body made for an interesting relationship.

Eventually, Josh realized he wasn't made out for the adult world. It was too much for him. He would rather return to being a normal twelve-year-old and grow up at a regular pace. So, he went back and found the same fortune-telling machine, made a wish, and became young again.

The movie *Big*, starring Tom Hanks, is a thought-provoking film. Coming of age films are a genre of film seeking to explain what it means to grow up. *Big* is one of the best examples. Films like this speak to each generation.

Big is one example among many coming-of-age films from the eighties. We could talk about films like *The Breakfast Club* or

Ferris Bueller's Day Off or *Better Off Dead.* Let's explore the coming of age for Generation Z.

So far we have studied the defining historical moments impacting Gen Z's worldview, like the Great Recession and the CO-VID-19 pandemic. We observed how secularism has shaped Gen Z's understanding of truth, identity, and sexuality. And we looked at how the smartphone changed the face of entertainment, shopping, and connecting with friends.

If we are to understand what it means to grow up today, we need to understand what growth is or is not taking place in today's youth. We also need to understand the stories Gen Z is told to model their lives after and the potentially tragic results.

ADULTING IN TODAY'S WORLD

I live in Portland, and one of the catchphrases people use to describe the city is "the city where Millennials come to retire." This means Portland is a place where many people come to extend "the good years" of their lives without settling down, getting married, or starting a family. Imagine a forty-year-old Millennial saying, "I'm sure I'll start a family when I grow up." That's Portland.

This sentiment is not just for Portland Millennials, it's also for members of Gen Z everywhere. Growing up in today's world as a teen is difficult. The story of Gen Z's development is tricky. It is not as simple as movies make it.

In *Big,* Josh experienced what it meant to be an adult and then desired to go back to childhood or adolescence. Many teens and young adults agree with Josh's desire today. In fact, the world today tells people to put off adulthood as much as possible. This is called *extended adolescence.*[1]

In simple terms, the three core stages of human development are childhood, adolescence, and adulthood. Adolescence correlates with the teenage years. So, the idea of extended adolescence means the teenage years stretched beyond what would be

---

1. Twenge, *iGen,* 17–47.

considered traditional ages. One way to measure the extension of the teenage years is to look at traditional milestones of maturity. These milestones are things like:

- Driving
- Dating
- Leaving home
- Jobs and financial independence
- Marriage and family

Sociologist Jean Twenge argues that these traditional milestones of adulthood first began to be delayed by young Gen Xers. From her studies, it was in the 1990s that members of Gen X began to postpone getting married, having children, and starting a career.[2] These trends have certainly continued with Gen Z. What we are seeing is a continual prolonging of the time between the beginning of adulthood and the attainment of these milestones of adulthood. It's not that someone does not want to drive or go on a date, but "just not yet." Maybe one day they will grow big. Let's look at each of these milestones.

Driving

Ferris Bueller's Day Off is another hit coming-of-age film from the eighties. Something clear in the film is that driving is viewed as the ultimate freedom of expression in high school. This has radically changed for Gen Z. Recent studies show that one in four members of Gen Z doesn't have a driver's license by their senior year of high school.[3] And they don't care.

There are many reasons behind this decrease. It has happened slowly over the last few decades. Teens point to several reasons. Perhaps they see their parent as a better driver. Many teens may

2. Twenge, *iGen*, 40.
3. Twenge, *iGen*, 26.

be afraid to fail the tests. Some argue they don't have anywhere important to be.

Driving is a great first milestone to look at because the change is observable. However, the reason behind the change is complex. This is true for all the milestones of adulthood. These changes make a huge impact on Gen Z's development.

Leaving Home

Another continued trend over the last several decades is never leaving their parents' home or the return to home after college. This trend reached a tipping point in 2014 when a study showed that more eighteen-to-thirty-four-year-olds were living with their parents instead of with a spouse or romantic partner.[4]

The reasons for this are complex. Finances do play a role. For example, the cost of living has increased in many areas of the US without a subsequent rise in salaries. One could also point to the student debt crisis. The average student is over $35,000 in debt by the time they are twenty-two years old. This makes the return to mom and dad alluring.

There are other reasons for this rise. The American cultural narrative of leaving home at eighteen is changing. For many, the teens and young adults of today may not feel like the rules of their parents' home prevent them from living the life they want to have. The end result is that there are fewer and fewer "empty nesters."

Jobs and Financial Independence

When my dad was twelve years old, he got his first job. He helped his father work as a milkman. They delivered fresh milk door to door around the town he grew up in. When my dad was twenty-two years old, his dad had passed away. My dad took over the milk delivery route on his own, looking to help provide for his mom and sisters.

4. Twenge, *iGen*, 222.

My dad did not seek a first job, it was assumed. The concept of financial independence may not have been on my dad's mind, but he sought it out by seeking to provide for himself and others.

Today, the job market looks different for teens. Studies show there are twice as many seniors in high school today without a job than there were seniors without a job two generations ago.[5] The downward trend in early employment does not mean a lack of career ambition in Generation Z. The desire to have a successful career is alive and well with this generation. The timing is just later.

Dating, Sex, Marriage, and Kids

Another major measurable milestone for adulthood is marriage and starting a family. Traditionally, these two have gone hand in hand. And what precedes marriage? Dating.

As with all of these milestones, there has been a decreasing trend of early dating among Gen Z. For example, as seniors in high school, 85 percent of Boomers had been on a date. Today it is only 50 percent for Gen Z.[6]

This is not because teens are simply less interested in one another. Instead, there has been a shift in relational connection through social media and the smartphone. There has been a decrease in the formality of a date because through the smartphone you have access to anyone, anywhere, anytime. There is also a decrease in teen sex (along with pregnancy). This could be due to the increased usage of pornography, along with an overall decrease in in-person social settings.

What do we know about marriage for Gen Z? These numbers are also projected to change. The average marrying age, if someone gets married at all, is being extended. In 1960, the average marrying age for a man was twenty-two years old, and for a woman it was twenty. Today, the average age for a man is twenty-nine

---

5. Twenge, *iGen*, 30.
6. Twenge, *iGen*, 40.

years old, and for a woman it's twenty-seven.[7] Similarly, studies are showing later and later dates for couples having children, if they have them at all.

These milestones of maturity are a great gauge to see a general societal trend. As mentioned, Gen Zers did not start these trends, but they are continuing them. Development is taking place at different stages of life for Gen Z.

If the movie *Big* were to be made today, it would be possible for Josh to go from twelve to twenty-five and still have no driver's license, no committed relationship, and be living with his parents. The movie could be called *Grad School*.

The story of Gen Z's coming of age is different from the stories of the past. Let's look at the coming-of-age films made for today's youth to see the differences.

GEN Z COMING OF AGE

The coming-of-age movies of today teach us about what it means to grow up Gen Z. These movies show how Gen Z is told to think about life, parents, dating, sex, and meaning. Key movies released like *To All the Boys I've Loved Before* or *Love, Simon* give a vivid depiction of what many in Gen Z feel and think.

In *To All the Boys I've Loved Before*, the female protagonist, Lara, writes secret love letters to all the boys she has loved. These letters were never intended to be sent out, but her little sister thought it would be fun to send them out for her. As with any good movie, chaos and love ensue. One of the recipients of the love letters does not want anyone to know he likes another girl; also Lara does not want the other guys to think she is still in love with them. They both decide to act like they are dating to throw people off the trail. After fake dating, Lara and her fake boyfriend eventually fall in love and make their relationship official.

In *Love, Simon*, Simon has a secret which nobody in his family or school knows. Simon is gay. Simon meets an anonymous

7. Seemiller and Grace, *Generation Z*, 108.

classmate online by his code name, Blue. Blue also admits he is gay and is hiding it from the school. This starts a journey of Simon searching for Blue and Simon beginning to share with people his true sexual identity. This whole journey is an emotional roller coaster with Simon eventually meeting Blue in person, and they begin dating.

These are the movies and stories that members of Generation Z are engaging with. When Gen Zers think of growing up, these stories are their models. They are told they must discover their sexuality, find their true identity, and protect themselves from the evil world. Their peers often tell them a plan of self-help and self-discovery. The movies always seem to end well, but movies are not real life. If these movies are models for the teens of today, let's understand the core problems they face in the world, the people they look to, and the unfortunate results.

The Problems

Every primary character in every story has a problem. Whether the story is a coming-of-age film or someone's true life, problems abound. As members of Generation Z process the world around them, two core problems come to the forefront of their lives: identity and safety. First, let's explore identity.

Identity. Finding one's identity is crucial in today's world. Stories Gen Z engage in make this focus abundantly clear. In the trailer for *To All the Boy's I've Loved Before*, there are two tag lines encouraging the audience to "find your courage" and to "write your destiny." Similarly, at the end of the trailer for *Love, Simon*, the voice of Simon says, "I'm done living in a world where I don't get to be who I am. I deserve a great love story." These movies continue the narrative of expressive individualism to their Gen Z audience. This narrative encourages people to find their true identity, meaning, and salvation through soul searching and self-discovery alone.

Many of the identity issues Gen Zers face stem from an understanding of how they define identity. Who am I? Why am I here? What is true? The cultural narrative of today forcefully combines identity and sexuality into one category. *Love, Simon* clearly states that finding one's true self means discovering and embracing one's true sexuality.

To take an even more popular movie, consider *Frozen 2*. *Frozen 2* is all about changing seasons of life.[8] It's a movie about the characters growing up and trying to figure out what it means to become an adult. How do you now make decisions? *Frozen 2* answers with a resounding "look inside of yourself."

The movies of today guide us on the path of secularism. The problem in many of these movies is not actually a problem of love but a problem of identity. The solution is often not external (ask the fortune-telling machine to make you small again), but internal (only you can free your true self). On the other hand, there is still perceived external danger in the world today.

Safety. Jonathan Haidt and Greg Lukianoff in their book *Coddling of the American Mind* observe a rise in what they call fragility and safetyism in the world today. They argue that Gen Z is being raised in a world where safety is the most important thing. Everything can hurt you: words, thoughts, and physical objects.

Haidt and Lukianoff observe that the world Boomers and Gen Xers grew up in was far more dangerous than the world Gen Zers are growing up in. In the US, crime began to increase around the 1960s and then leveled off in the 1990s and is now back to rates close to sixty years prior.[9] Still, the fear of crime did not decrease. Nor did the fear of injury and kidnapping decrease. The result is that we have parents who are overly fearful of their children's safety, even though the world they live in is significantly safer than the world the parents grew up in. This is a problem.

On top of a fear of risk for their children, the actions of protection from parents and others in authority teach children to consider themselves fragile. Therefore, children are less likely to take risks in life. Thus, they delay getting their driver's license, getting a job, and moving out. These are all risks.

8. Casteel, "Frozen 2."

9. Lukianoff and Haidt, *Coddling of the American Mind*, 167.

Additionally, Haidt and Lukianoff observe that safety is no longer only physical safety. Today its physical *and* emotional safety. As we see in many of the coming-of-age movies of today, the world is a difficult place to live. People say things that really hurt, and many Gen Zers are not prepared for it.[10]

The Guides: Parents

In many Gen Z films, friends and parents guide the protagonist through the problems they face. The guides tell the characters to look within and do what feels good, and then they will overcome their problems. Often these parents and friends do not offer external truth or wisdom to solve the character's issues. Yet, we all know parents are incredibly important. Gen Z knows this too. You can scarcely find a teen who does not look to parents for advice and guidance. Sadly, too often parents do not make good guides in life. Why is this?

First, not all parents are actively involved in the lives of their children. According to research, only three in five members of Gen Z live in a house with two married parents.[11]

Second, many parents aim to be friends with their children rather than authority figures. In *To All the Boys I've Loved Before*, Lara's dad offers little guidance in life other than a pack of condoms. Her father's advice is not too different from her friends' advice. Parents are afraid to guide their children and would rather reduce their relationship to a friendship.

Third, parents are double-minded.[12] They are both overprotective *and* under protective. In many areas of life, parents could be categorized as helicopter parents who hover over every detail of a kid's life, while at the same time being completely hands-off in other crucial areas. The hands-off area for many parents is the digital world. Over the last several decades there has been a rise in

---

10. Lukianoff and Haidt, *Coddling of the American Mind*, 163–79.

11. Seemiller and Grace, *Generation Z*, 103.

12. *Gen Z: The Culture*, 34.

protecting children and teens from the harsh world around them while at the same time letting them roam free in a digital world. Parents are ignoring the single most shaping aspect of their children's lives. Parents are quick to protect their children from the outside world, but they have been slow to protect their children where it matters most: the world on the web. The impact of one far outweighs the other.

The Tragic Results

Growing up Gen Z is not easy. The secular world preaches that they are the solution to their own problems. Technology says they can do anything with a smartphone in their hand. The guides in their life protect them from things they may not need protection from, while letting them roam free with addictive content. What is the result?

Anxiety and depression.

Rates of depression and anxiety have increased dramatically among American teens. Today, one out of every seven women in the US believes she has a psychological disorder.[13] The growth of anxiety and depression is a deadly cycle.

Studies have directly linked amount of screen time, internet usage, and social media to unhappiness. Additionally, Jean Twenge speaks of several studies that found a direct link between social media usage and unhappiness, worry, sadness, anger, loneliness, and depression.[14] These studies show the risk to be highest in younger teens. Other studies show that younger females are in the worst situation.[15]

The numbers are increasing and do not seem to be waning. Many of these studies took place before the pandemic. Unfortunately, I fear the mental health of teens and young adults only worsened as a result of further isolation. On top of this, many in

---

13. Lukianoff and Haidt, *Coddling of the American Mind*, 157.

14. Twenge, *iGen*, 78–79.

15. Lukianoff and Haidt, *Coddling of the American Mind*, 149.

Gen Z do not have adequate guides to help them through the pain. This generation needs hope.

So, the very thing Gen Zers have been groomed to run to is the very thing hurting them the most. Growing up slowly in a secularized, technology-filled world is not the utopia it promised to be. What hope can be offered to those in Gen Z? And how do they cope? And how can the Lord use them?

MISFITS AND UNDERDOGS

At this point you may be thinking: what is God going to do? They are secular. They are addicted to technology. They aren't even growing up. They are totally unprepared for life. But let me tell you, these are exactly the people God uses. God has always desired to use the young, the misfit, the underdog, the under-skilled, weak, and unprepared. Just look at examples throughout Scripture:

- Jacob, the younger brother, was chosen over his brother, Esau.
- Joseph was sold into slavery because his older brothers hated him so much. Later he became second in command in Egypt and wielded his power to save his brothers and family.
- David was the youngest brother and seen to be unfit as a King, but the Lord chose him.
- Ruth was a young woman outside of the tribe of Israel whom God used to maintain the line of Jesus.
- Jeremiah said he was too young to speak, but then God made him a great prophet.
- Jesus' twelve disciples were teenagers from a small village few people cared about.
- Peter was a loud-mouthed and brash young man. Yet the Lord built the early church on him.

So often the way we think about engaging Gen Z is about forming the smartest, most competent, and highest achieving members of society possible. But the Lord's ways are not our ways.

The Lord loves these redemptive reversals. He can do the same with this generation that so many misunderstand and underrate!

Gen Zers are unique in their upbringing and unique in their motivations. Let's see how the world they live in has impacted their motivations.

REFLECTION: BRIDGING THE GAP

1. Ask yourself, in terms of the traditional milestones of adulthood, how was your generation different from the generation before you?

2. Ask Gen Zers what they see as traditional milestones of adulthood. At what age do they expect to pursue these milestones?

3. Ask Gen Zers in what ways they have seen screen time positively and negatively affect their lives. Do they think it has an impact on mental health?

6

Misfits' Motivations

It happened so fast. I was driving, enjoying the music and conversation with my wife. Then a car sped past me, cutting me off.

More specifically, *someone* cut me off. Now it's personal.

Immediately, I snapped out of my joyful mood and turned angry. I shouted, "Hey man! Slow down! There's a speed limit! Don't you know there are kids in the cars you are flying by!"

Of course, they were going twenty-five miles per hour faster than me, so they heard nothing and took no interest in my dismay.

Just then, I realized something: I judge others' actions without knowing their motivations, whereas I judge my actions only by my motivations.

What do I mean? Well, if someone speeds past you, you become angry at their action. If you speed past someone, you had a good reason—maybe you needed to get home because of a sporting event. If you're on the phone while driving, you're getting directions. If someone else is on the phone while driving, you hope they're getting a ticket. Do you see what's happening? You judge others' actions without knowing their motivations. But when you assess your actions, your motivations are pure. We all do it.

Let's examine the motivations, not actions, of Gen Z. When all we do is judge actions and behaviors, we miss the story. Motivations help broaden our understanding of people and situations.

Why was the person speeding? Why were you on your phone? Why was your friend late to your party? More importantly, why do Gen Zers behave the way they do?

We have examined the world of Gen Z. Clearly we've seen how the world Gen Zers live in impacts their motivations. They live in a secular world run by technology. It's a world where the very definition of growing up is changing. The world Gen Zers inhabit is telling them to determine their identity through finding their own personal truth, which is often linked to their sexuality. Gen Zers live in a world with limitless content and limitless connection at all times. They live in a world telling them to extend the best years of their lives before they become an adult. We must first understand the motivations of Gen Zers, then we can understand the actions of this generation of misfits and dreamers.

Let's peek behind the curtain of Gen Zers' motivations. What makes them tick? Why do they make the decisions they make in life, relationships, and careers? I want to see the strengths of these motivations and then identify the pitfalls. We'll also explore how each of these motivations leaves room for the Christ-followers in Gen Z to grow further in their Christian walk. When it comes to what motivates Gen Z, there are four primary motivations: connection, caution, causes, and customization.

Connection: Let's Be Friends

Generation Z is the most connected generation to ever live. Often, this idea is forgotten when people suppose Gen Z is not relational because of the amount of screen time they rack up. However, Gen Z values connection. Also, Gen Zers are really good at leveraging the connections they have.

It often seems easy for older generations to look down on younger generations about their screen time. Many say, "Hang up and hang out!" However, for many in Gen Z, hanging out with friends is precisely what they are doing while on their screens!

In the world today, students can go to school and have a conversation with a friend. They get home and continue the same conversation online. Then they continue the conversation the next day at school. Smartphones and social media have changed, and even *enhanced*, community for Gen Zers. They live in a world where parents and friends can track locations at all times and message them about their whereabouts—and many love it. Simply put, Gen Zers are deeply relational, and they love connecting with friends and family.

Yet there are pitfalls for Gen Z to navigate when it comes to connection. Here are the concerns.

First, Gen Z is easily addicted to the quick connection made through social media. What begins to happen over time is people begin to be *used* by social media, rather than people *using* social media. We must learn how to use social media as a tool with a purpose in our life rather than the purpose of our life.

Second, social media can make Gen Z's world too small. The internet allows people to have interest-based relationships. The pro is all these interest-based relationships can spread around the world, and you control what you do, what you see, and who you talk to. The con is we choke out different interests, different voices, and different opinions. If you're a Republican, then you can only follow Republicans. If you're a Democrat, you can only follow Democrats. If you believe in global warming, you only follow people who believe in global warming. Reformed can only follow Reformed and woke can only follow woke. Social media makes Gen Z, and everyone, insular in their relationships.

Third, Gen Z's longing for online connection can lead to loneliness and social anxiety. When it's second nature to connect with your friends in small segments of time scattered throughout the day, it is difficult to spend extended, intentional time with others. When little digital touches here and there become the norm, extended times with people in social settings can become overwhelming. As a result, some members of Gen Z will continue to pull back from social settings and groups, leading to further isolation. It is disheartening to realize that the generation with the most potential for connection can easily squander relationships by reducing them to clicks, likes, and shares.

Though there are pitfalls in Gen Z's desire for connection, we need to remember God created people for relationship! All of humanity is created for relationship with God and for relationship with one another. Whether a member or mentor of Gen Z, how do we help Gen Zers think well about connections? Involvement in a local church is the best place to start. God has given believers a unique community through the local church, and this should not be neglected (Heb 10:24–25). This will be covered more in later chapters.

In fact, Gen Zers can use their connection for great good. Shawn, a college freshman I met, is a great example. He was tall and athletic. He was easy to chat with and was thinking of entering the medical field. I met him in Minneapolis and asked him what he used his social media for. He told me he was an influencer for Jesus on TikTok.

I wasn't sure what he meant. I asked Shawn, "What do you mean? How many followers do you have?"

Shawn said, "I have around eight hundred."

I said, "Eight hundred . . . not bad" (not knowing if that's good or bad).

Shawn said, "No. I meant eight hundred thousand. I have eight hundred thousand followers on TikTok."

I was in awe! Shawn is more connected at nineteen than anyone I know at any age or stage in life. One post from Shawn is the equivalent of speaking to multiple stadiums filled with people.

Don't count Gen Z out! Gen Zers are connected, desiring to make more connections, and some are wanting to use their platforms to make Jesus known. Let's encourage more!

Caution: Fear of Failure

In most areas of life, being cautious is a good thing. I want a child to be cautious not careless when crossing a road. I want a surgeon to be cautious not careless when operating. Caution leads to making safe decisions in difficult situations. Caution can be critical.

Life in today's world is viewed as one giant difficult decision. Gen Z seeks to approach this decision with extreme caution. Caution describes the way Gen Z thinks about careers, the job market, social media, and everyday risks.

Caution stems from Gen Z's upbringing and the extension of adolescence. One key defining moment affecting Gen Zers' motivation of caution is the Great Recession of 2008–2009 and its aftermath. Gen Zers had a front row seat to family members losing jobs, homes, and retirement funds. They saw the world and the economy spiral downward. They, at a young age, learned the world could hit you and your family hard. The result? These events led to fear of the unknown and a cautious outlook on the world.

This focus on caution has led Gen Z to a high level of pragmatism and practical thinking. This is revealed as Gen Zers think through college and careers. I frequently encounter students studying business, accounting, computer science, or engineering not because they love these topics, but because they believe these degrees will lead to successful, stable careers. Additionally, I continue to meet students who follow a less traditional approach to school. To keep their debt costs down many students opt for community college the first two years of school and then work slowly through the remainder of the degree at a larger university. Students may decide to take college classes throughout high school, so they can keep their time at college to a minimum, thus reducing debt.

To be sure, Gen Z's caution can lead to a lack of ambition. Often, however, it leads to more practical solutions to life problems. An example could be how Gen Z approaches financial goals. In 2021, when the US government granted pandemic stimulus checks to many US citizens, Gen Z took a different approach from older adults. Many young people did not go out and buy something extravagant or unneeded. Instead, they saved it. They paid off debt.[1]

Caution does not simply impact jobs, careers, and finances, it impacts the way Gen Z thinks about social media. A young businesswoman named Justine Sacco boarded a flight from the UK to South Africa. Before putting her phone into airplane mode

1. Chavez, "Gimme the Stimmy!"

for the eleven-hour flight, Justine fired off one quick tweet to her followers: "Going to Africa. Hope I don't get AIDS. Just kidding. I'm white!"[2] By the time Justine landed eleven hours later, her tweet had become the number one trending item on Twitter with a hashtag to follow: "#HasJustineLandedYet." Unbeknownst to her, while she was in the air, the entire world was set ablaze with comments about her tweet, and they demanded her employer fire her. By the time she landed, her phone had hundreds of messages, along with her employer stating her termination.[3] It's stories like these that impact the way Gen Z cautiously views their digital life. As a result, Gen Z opts for private and filtered social media use.

Gen Zers are cautious when it comes to careers. They are cautious when it comes to social media. They are also cautious in the everyday risks of life. Sociologist Jean Twenge confirms Gen Z is less rebellious than previous generations and more risk averse.[4] Gen Z is less likely to drink underaged, less likely to do drugs, and less likely to have teen pregnancy. Caution pays off.

Gen Z's motivation of caution and risk aversion is complex. There are obvious strengths to cautious decisions. There are pitfalls too. Gen Zers may be tempted to miss out on the life experiences of college to save money. They may miss out on fun, life-giving events because they wanted to avoid taking a step to meet a group of new people in person.

As Christians desiring to see Gen Z know Jesus and make him known, what does it mean for us to help them have faith and take the right risks? According to Jesus, following him is risky. In Luke 14, Jesus tells a parable to his disciples to illustrate the cost of discipleship. He says, "Whoever does not bear his own cross and come after me cannot be my disciple. For which of you, desiring to build a tower, does not first sit down and count the cost, whether he has enough to complete it?" (Luke 14:27–28). There is a cost to following Jesus. We must consider the cost before following him.

2. The original tweet has been deleted but can be seen in Ronson, "One Stupid Tweet."
3. Ronson, "One Stupid Tweet."
4. Twenge, *iGen*, 3.

The answer to seeing members of Gen Z come to Jesus is not a misinformed, shallow, and no-action easy-to-believe message. We are correct to communicate that repentance and faith in Jesus is risky. But this is a risk worth taking! Jesus has invited all people, all generations to risk following him.

CAUSES: CHAMPIONS FOR CHANGE

"How dare you? You have stolen my dreams and my childhood with your empty words." These are words spoken to the United Nations by a seventeen-year-old Swedish girl named Greta Thunberg.[5] What did she address the UN about? Climate change and carbon emissions produced by big businesses and big governments. Four months after addressing the UN, *Time Magazine* named Greta the 2019 Person of the Year![6]

Regardless of your thoughts on climate change, Greta's words will give you pause. What gives a young, seventeen-year-old girl the wherewithal to speak to world leaders so forcefully? Greta cares about the environment. Greta is a champion for change. She is not alone.

Gen Z is a deeply cause-oriented and philanthropic generation. One report even called them "philanthroteens." Why "philanthroteens"? There are stories of Gen Z members like Jack Andraka, who left school at fifteen to work on a simple test to detect pancreatic cancer. Or stories like that of Mary Grace Henry, who started a business to help fund Ugandan girls' education.[7] The list is endless. The top causes Gen Z fights for typically revolve around environmental and social justice issues.

One reason Gen Zers care so much is because they are so connected! Social media is a perfect place for this generation to discover causes and to show the world what they care for. If you follow them on social media, you will see many of them post things

5. Rosenblatt, "Greta Thunberg Lambasts World Leaders."
6. Alter et al., "Greta Thunberg."
7. Meade, "'Philanthroteens.'"

they care about. They don't just post about their trip to a store, or a new car, or a picture of their dessert. They post about causes with an understanding of social change. However, there are pitfalls in Gen Z's desire to champion causes.

First, because of the nature of the internet and social media, Gen Z can quickly back issues undeserving of support. Think back to the Wayfair child trafficking conspiracy theory. Yes, child trafficking is a horrible, but Wayfair is not at the center of this trafficking—no matter how many times it's shared and re-shared online by Gen Z.

Second, because of the constant access to causes online, Gen Z can become either numb to or overwhelmed by the problems in this world. One can only see so many new stories about a war on the other side of the world before becoming numb. From a biblical perspective, Christians must learn to care for what is happening in the world, especially the areas closest to them, while trusting in the Lord's providence and sovereignty.

As Christians, Gen Z's focus on causes should be a source of great hope! Gen Z cares about injustices in the world. So does God! God is a God who loves justice.

If a member of Gen Z is a Christian, we would do well to help them think biblically and theologically about the social issues they support. We should point them to the Bible and what it has to say about God's justice and judgment on evil (Deut 16:18–20; Ps 33:5; Mic 6:8; Isa 42:1–3). If a member of Gen Z is not a Christian, justice is a wonderful way to bring up the topic of evil and sin in the world. There is injustice because of the evil of sin, and everyone is sinful. Using the causes Gen Z cares about is a perfect way to transition to God's example of sacrificial love and justice through the cross of Christ.

CUSTOMIZATION: ON-DEMAND LIFESTYLE

When my wife was a child, she went to a Build-a-Bear Workshop. It's a store specializing in helping children build their own teddy bear. Kids can choose the color of fur, the eyes, the clothes, and even the sounds it makes when squeezed. You get the opportunity to customize your new favorite toy. It's a novel idea.

Gen Z lives in a world where virtually everything is customizable. Because of the internet and social media, the options for customization make going to a Build-a-Bear Workshop look like child's play. From your online profile to your favorite pictures, to coffee and food orders, everything can be customized. It's true all of these options are available to anyone alive today, but it's different if you were raised this way.

Customization may not be the word Gen Z uses often, but it's a power they constantly wield. Gen Z does not simply have the ability to customize parts of their life, it's become a motivating factor for life. This has become clear when thinking about colleges and degree programs. Students may choose a school where they can study exactly what they think is best. When it comes to hiring Gen Z after college, they will trend to choosing the job with the most flexible and customizable benefits package and hours. Customization is king.

The potential pitfalls of Gen Z's motivation to customize are many. First, customization can be overwhelming. Though people desire to customize in life, it's a daunting task. When you were a child, you would simply watch whatever your parents told you to watch. As an adult we choose from a thousand channels and devices. Eventually, decision paralysis sets in. Not being able to decide on a movie is hardly an issue, but what about your major in college? Or your career? Or which benefits package you want at work? For a cautious and stress-prone generation, customizations like these lead to further stress and anxiety.

Second, customization is unrealistic in every area of life. The ability to customize more and more parts of life leads people to believe they can customize every part of life. In fact, many students believe they can customize the perfect plan for life from the time they are twenty to the time they die. They have the plan for the perfect spouse, the perfect house, the perfect job, and the perfect vacation. Social media only reinforces these ideas.

Third, customization puts self at the center. A life full of tinkering and customizing puts you, your plans, and your comfort at the center of life. Constant curation makes you think you are the only authority in life. Nobody can tell you how to live. Expressive individualism, the secular world, and customization go hand in hand. This pitfall of customization opposes the biblical worldview and what it means to follow Jesus.

As Christians seeking to see Gen Z know Jesus and make him known, we must understand Gen Z's motivation to customize and curate. This motivation may be more clear to parents and those with close relationships to Gen Zers. Parents may see their children ask for more control over everyday life: food choices, fun options, and school activities. For pastors and ministers, you may see this motivation of customization show up in your leaders. They may want more say or more flexibility and options in their leadership roles. Instead of simply following what an authority figure chooses, members of Gen Z tend to share what they desire. This desire to customize is not necessarily a bad or sinful thing, but it is something those interacting with Gen Z need to recognize and interact with on a healthy level.

Ultimately, like all of us, Christian members of Gen Z need to grow in their understanding of sacrifice and service. Jesus is our model through his sacrificial death on the cross for the sins of the world. He says, "For even the Son of Man came not to be served but to serve, and to give his life as a ransom for many" (Mark 10:45). Jesus actively served during his ministry and always sought to do the will of his father. Jesus did not customize his way to the cross, he obediently followed the path before him. Before the cross, Jesus clearly put the will of the Father above his own will (Luke 22:42).

We must help Christian members of Gen Z understand Jesus' sacrifice and service and the New Testament's charge to believers to seek the interest of others above themselves (Phil 2:3–4). With a gospel-focused lens, their motivation to customize will not be a stumbling block to faith but an ability to serve fellow Christians, and uniquely reach out to non-Christians for the glory of Christ.

Gen Z is motivated by connection, caution, causes, and customization. It is clear these motivations can be fuel for a Christ-glorifying life. If Gen Zers' motivations shift from a focus on self to a focus on God and sharing his love with the world around them, then they will be a powerful force. What can older generations say or do to care for this generation of misfits and dreamers? It starts with a compassionate heart. Let's cultivate one.

REFLECTION: BRIDGING THE GAP

1. Ask yourself, have you sought to understand the impact of the world on the motivations of Gen Z?

2. Ask Gen Zers what big decisions they have coming up. Are they stressed, scared, or prepared make the decision?

3. Ask Gen Zers what causes they desire to support and what causes are worthy of support.

7

A Compassionate Heart

JORDAN WAS WHAT MANY consider a typical member of Gen Z. He wanted to live for something big, but he was from a small town nobody had ever heard of. He got his first phone at twelve, and it changed the game for him. It reinvented the way he spent time with (or without) friends and the way he connected with the world outside his small town.

Like many in Gen Z, he was a good student in high school. He wanted to work hard on assignments because he wanted to avoid failing school. He was practical and cautious toward the challenges of life. Jordan knew the job market was a competitive place. He wanted to go to a good university to get a leg up on life.

In the midst of working so hard for school and then connecting with people on social media, who has time for a girlfriend? Not Jordan. Though I'm sure his parents wanted him to meet a nice girl, he just wasn't interested.

Not only did Jordan put off getting a girlfriend, he put many of his extracurricular activities on hold too. He was part of the all-state choir at his school. He had a fantastic voice. Jordan quit choir. Track team? He quit that too. Why would he quit these activities? Well, he just couldn't juggle everything he needed to juggle.

In college, it was more of the same for Jordan. He chose to start at one school, then quickly transferred. At the new school he decided he didn't want to be in person, but he wanted to be an online student. He moved back home to live with his parents. Jordan seems to be like what most older generations think of Gen Z.

At this point you might think to yourself: "Yep, this is typical Gen Z. He's not growing up, he is scared of commitment, and he's for sure a slacker." Would you give up on a Jordan if he was your son or in your church?

Regardless of the world, motivations, and challenges this generation faces, we *can* control our response to them. In a world fraught with division, can older generations learn to unite with and care well for Gen Z? Can we bridge the gap between generations with compassion? Jesus viewed people through a different lens than many. Peter was a stubborn young man, but Jesus saw the future of the church in him. Jesus did not condemn but was moved to compassion. With the Jordans of this generation, if we move from condemnation to compassion, we may be surprised what the second half of the story looks like.

DEFINITION OF COMPASSION

When I think of compassion, I think of Jesus. *Splanchnizomai* is the Greek verb meaning "to have compassion" or "to be moved to compassion." It stems from the Greek noun for intestine. How are intestine and compassion related? To be moved to compassion is to have your insides moved to pity for someone else. Compassion is a gut reaction.

In the Gospels, we see Jesus' compassion lead him to action. This is what compassion does. When Jesus saw the needs of others, his gut reaction was to feel compassion and step into action. Wouldn't it be nice for our compassion to be a gut reaction? Unfortunately, many people's gut reaction toward Gen Z is not one of compassion. Sadly, it's condemnation.

For most Millennials, Gen Xers, and Boomers, all they have is condemnation for Gen Z. But it's a one-way road. One researcher said in his studies that he found the mudslinging to be one-directional. The older seem to condemn the younger while the younger speak more charitably of the older.[1] But Jesus looked at the people he ministered to and he had compassion.

One of the most clear examples of Jesus' compassion is in Matt 9:36–37:

> And Jesus went throughout all the cities and villages, teaching in their synagogues and proclaiming the gospel of the kingdom and healing every disease and every affliction. When he saw the crowds, *he had compassion* for them, because they were harassed and helpless, like sheep without a shepherd. (Emphasis added.)

Jesus did many things during his three years of ministry. He traveled, taught, and did miracles, but he always took time to see the crowds. In the midst of his busyness, he was still moved to compassion toward people. He had compassion like a shepherd toward his sheep. Shepherds must be tender and ever vigilant to the flock.

I recently saw a video of a shepherd helping a sheep wedged in a hole. As soon as the sheep is pulled from the hole, it jumps three times and lands right back in the hole. Stuck until the shepherd saves it again. Over and over again the shepherd's compassion and care for the sheep led to action. The same is true for Jesus!

Multiple times throughout the Gospels, we see Jesus moved to compassion, then act. Before the feeding of the five thousand, Jesus is moved to compassion for the great crowd, and he heals their sick (Matt 14:14; Mark 6:34). In the feeding of the four thousand, Jesus is moved to compassion toward the crowd who have been with him three days without food. Out of his compassion he multiplies food for the crowds (Matt 15:32; Mark 8:2). Another time, Jesus heals a boy tormented with an unclean spirit because of his compassion (Mark 9:22). Furthermore, out of compassion, Jesus raises a widow's son from the dead (Luke 7:13).

Jesus and the Father are one (John 10:30). And the Father is frequently spoken of as compassionate and gracious (Exod 34:6; Neh 9:31; Jonah 4:2; Ps 103:8). Throughout Scripture, we see the

---

1. Kinnaman and Matlock, *Faith for Exiles*, 120.

compassionate and gracious God engage with his people. Jesus loved and engaged with those who had needs. He taught his disciples to do the same. As we think about engaging with and loving Gen Z, what can we learn from the Shepherd and Overseer of our souls? (1 Pet 2:25).

CULTIVATING COMPASSIONATE DISCIPLESHIP

Compassion is not our natural bent—especially toward those different from us. We understand the value of engaging with Gen Z, but perhaps we need help growing our heart in working with this promising generation. From the example of Jesus, let me provide four action steps to cultivate a compassionate heart toward Gen Z. First, we need to understand our need for compassion. Second, we must pray. Third, we need to initiate with this generation. And finally, we must anticipate the obstacles.

Understand Your Need

In order to first cultivate a compassionate heart for Gen Z, we need to understand the compassion the Lord has shown us. Throughout the Gospels, like in Matthew 9, Jesus often speaks of sheep and shepherds. This is fitting. Jesus becomes a sacrificial sheep for his people so that he may rise from the grave and become their Shepherd. Isaiah beautifully prophesies Jesus as the sacrificial lamb:

> All we like sheep have gone astray; we have turned—every one—to his own way; and the Lord has laid on him the iniquity of us all. He was oppressed, and he was afflicted, yet he opened not his mouth; like a lamb that is led to the slaughter, and like a sheep that before its shearers is silent, so he opened not his mouth. (Isa 53:6–7)

Everyone one of us without Christ is a wandering sheep. We are lost, for all eternity, apart from the help of the Lord. Jesus became a sacrificial lamb for our sins, for our waywardness, that we might be set free. We are set free to follow Jesus as our Shepherd.

Our greatest need in cultivating a heart of compassion is to understand the compassion poured out on us through the gospel. Jesus' death brings us life. Jesus' resurrection gives us hope to share his compassion to the ends of the earth. So, as you begin to pray for, initiate with, and empower this promising generation, do not lose sight of the wonderful compassion the Lord has first given you. Compassion toward you should manifest compassion from you!

We Must Pray

As mentioned, Matt 9:36–37 displays Jesus showing compassion on the crowds. There is another key observation. Jesus does not simply see the needs of the crowd and fix the needs himself. Jesus turns to his disciples and makes the whole situation a teaching moment.

In Matt 9:38 Jesus says, "The harvest is plentiful, but the laborers are few; therefore pray earnestly to the Lord of the harvest to send out laborers into his harvest."

What was Jesus' solution to the problems of the world? Prayer. Jesus' solution was not for him to move faster so that he might personally have compassion on all the people of the earth. Jesus' solution was to empower his people to pray.

Prayer is powerful. Prayer has the power to both transform your heart and the world around you. We need the power of prayer to humble us before the Lord and teach us how to engage and empower Gen Z. What are some practical ways for you to pray for Gen Z?

First, pray for the Gen Z members you've already initiated with! Pray for tangible moments of engagement and opportunities for compassion. If you don't already have close relationships with any members of Gen Z, pray the Lord would provide someone for you to invest in.

Second, pray for your heart toward this generation. Gen Z may be quite a bit different from you. Perhaps its members grew up at a different time and have different motivations. Ask the Lord to give you a compassionate heart toward this generation. Don't just stop by praying for yourself. Pray also for your family, your school, your church, or your organization as well.

Third, pray for ways to multiply ministry among Gen Zers. Just like Jesus turned to his disciples and asked them to pray about a larger impact in the world around them, you too should pray the Lord would multiply the impact of Gen Z. Pray for Christian Gen Z leaders to rise up and to help their Gen Z friends come to know Jesus and make an impact on the world.

Initiate with This Generation

From the example of Jesus we learn we must initiate with the surrounding needs. As soon as a need was made aware to him, he engaged. Remember, compassion is a gut reaction to lovingly engage with someone. Jesus initiated with the people around him, and so should we!

If you are a Christian reading this, the Lord has already worked mightily in your life. The Lord has given you wisdom from his Spirit. Now we must desire to impart the wisdom and make an impact on those younger than us. It can be easy for cultural and generational difference to stop us from engaging, but this generation needs to hear the good news of the gospel of Jesus just as much as any other. Proclamation of the gospel and discipleship as Christians takes direct initiation from older generations.

I'm not only reminded by how Jesus engaged with the needs of people around him, but also by how Jesus initiated with his disciples. Jesus told his disciples to "follow me" over and over throughout the Gospels. The initial call is not the only place. He reminds his followers over and again the need and cost of following him (Matt 8:22; 10:38; 16:24).

Our initiation with Gen Z is meeting them where they are. Our invitation is also discipling them to grow in their knowledge of God's character, the gospel, and their role as church members and ambassadors of Christ to the world. If you know members of Gen Z who follow Jesus, help them grow in their faith. If you don't know members of Gen Z who follow Jesus, be faithful in proclaiming the good news of the gospel to them.

To Jesus, the needs of the people around him were clear. For us, maybe the needs of Gen Zers are not so obvious. So, we need to grow in our ability to initiate with them. Let me give two practical steps in initiating with Gen Z.

First, ask questions! We must ask Gen Zers questions to learn more about their experience in today's world. Often we lack compassion because we don't understand the problems someone else is facing.

Second, use additional resources to grow your cultural IQ. Axis is a phenomenal organization focusing on connecting parents, teens, and Jesus in a disconnected world (www.axis.org). Axis has a weekly email named *The Cultural Translator* that gives important cultural insight. The appendix at the back of this book will have a list of other books to read.

Not only should we seek to initiate with members of Gen Z, but we should also help them navigate the obstacles of life.

Anticipate the Obstacles

Compassion does not mean everything will be easy. In order to cultivate a compassionate heart, we must anticipate the issues and obstacles Gen Z faces in following Jesus. Obstacles are meant to be navigated. As someone seeking to cultivate a compassionate heart for Gen Z, you are to help them navigate the obstacles in their lives.

An unhelpful phrase I often hear older Christians use when they reflect on younger generations is what I call "back in my day" statements. *Back in my day*, we got our driver's license at sixteen! *Back in my day* we sat through Sunday school, church service, and never had a phone to distract us. *Back in my day* people were married at eighteen, with a full-time job. *Back in my day* I could pay for college as I went. *Back in my day* living at home after college wasn't an option.

Though many "back in my day" statements are true, they never foster a sense of compassion. Statements like these can even drive a wedge between you and your audience. The truth is, each generation can have a "back in my day" statement. Each generation faces different obstacles in life. It's an opportunity for some cross-generational learning.

Paul, in his first letter to the church of Thessalonica, urges the church to have a loving and compassionate heart toward their brothers and sisters in Christ, saying, "And we urge you, brothers, admonish the idle, encourage the fainthearted, help the weak, be patient with them all" (1 Thess 5:14).

As we think about the challenges Gen Z faces, this short list is a beautiful picture of shepherding, discipleship, and leading Gen Z today.

- Admonish the idle
- Encourage the fainthearted
- Help the weak
- Be patient with them all

As we think through those members of Generation Z who are in our lives, are they idle or lazy? Are they fainthearted or timid? Are they weak? For each person there will be obstacles to following Jesus, and our role is to love them well by caring for them well. For some in Generation Z, they need to be admonished. For some in Generation Z, they need to be encouraged and comforted. For some in Generation Z, they need to be helped when they are weak. For everybody, always, they need patience. Too often when we deal with others who are younger, or older, than us, there is an undercurrent of impatience. Paul reminds us to be patient with every person, regardless of where they are.

As we move from compassion to empowerment, we are to shepherd and lead well—always pointing back to the true Shepherd of our souls. As we point people to Jesus, we should point them to the things Jesus cared about. We need to invest in this generation because the Lord desires to use it for his glory.

Remember Jordan from the opening story of this chapter? Well, you only heard part of the story.

Jordan Whitmer is certainly a proud member of Gen Z. He also is a typical member of Gen Z. There is one difference, though. The Lord has worked mightily through Jordan's gifting, opportunities, and relationships to enable him to be a strong gospel witness to members of Gen Z around the world.

All the elements of Jordan's story above were actually factors helping him start the HowToLife Movement (www.howtolifemovement.com), a global movement focused on reaching members of Gen Z for Christ. A group dreaming to see other misfit members of Gen Z follow Jesus!

For Jordan it all started in high school. Jordan and some friends saw a gospel need in their high school. Evangelism was a cause they wanted to get behind. Jordan leveraged every social media contact he could and held the first HowToLife event. Over seven hundred high school students from his school and the surrounding area came. Jordan was from a small town but wanted to make a big impact.

This first event led to many more. And these events explain many of the decisions Jordan made in high school and going into college. Why did Jordan drop out of all-state choir? He needed more time to focus on HowToLife. Why had Jordan not been on a date? He saw what he was doing as far more important than finding a girlfriend. Why is Jordan constantly on his phone and social media? The HowToLife Movement rises and falls on social media. Why did Jordan change schools and move home? So he could finish college faster and travel more for the movement.

In the first six years of its ministry, the HowToLife Movement has held over ninety events in twenty states and six countries. Digitally, it has had an impact with youth in over forty countries! This is social media used for the glory of God.

What many condemn as "ordinary Gen Z behavior," such as living at home, never dating, and always being on their phone, Jordan has used for extraordinary impact. In fact, Jordan told me, "If Gen Z can truly come to believe God can use them, then the whole world would be reached in ten years." Long live the misfits and dreamers.

Having a compassionate heart enables us to see the potential in this generation. If we understand our need for compassion, pray, initiate, and anticipate obstacles to growth, we can see more Jordans! The Lord desires to use and reach every generation. How do we get members of Gen Z to turn into Jordans? It starts with a compassion heart and moves to an invitation. Let's look at the invitation of Scripture.

REFLECTION: BRIDGING THE GAP

1. Ask yourself, in what specific ways can you pray for Gen Zers in your life?

2. Ask yourself, what is the next step you need to take in order to initiate with Gen Z?

3. Ask Gen Zers in what ways they have seen older generations lack compassion for Gen Z.

8

A Trans-generational Narrative

GROWING UP I WANTED to make my mark on history. I wanted to live a life story others longed to imitate. From a young age, I was always looking for meaning. For some reason, I tied my meaning to my grown-up job. As a kid I wanted to be a firefighter, then a Lego engineer, then a professional skateboarder, then a pro gamer, then the next Michael Phelps.

I was constantly reminded how boring my story was. I realized a Lego engineer wasn't a real job, professional skateboarders are crazier than I am, and that nobody would be impressed with a pro gamer. My final realization was that Michael Phelps is a freak of nature and nobody can compete with someone like him. I figured my story wasn't destined to matter.

Entering my senior year of high school, I was on a search for significance, but I was coming up dry. At the beginning of the first semester, someone asked me a strange question: "Have you ever read the story of Scripture?"

To which I responded, "Do you mean the Bible? Like the whole thing? All the pages?"

As an eighteen-year-old, and someone who had grown up in a Christian home I still couldn't fathom someone reading the entire Bible. I'm sure there were people who did, but they were probably locked in a monastery on the side of a mountain. It didn't seem worth my time. There was no way it was interesting or engaging. Why would I read it?

Then my friend said, "Yes, the Bible. I challenge you to read the entire Bible. Beginning to end. It only takes three or four chapters a day for a year. I bet you'll change your mind on what you think about it."

I accepted his challenge. I began in Genesis and began to read three to four chapters a day, just as my friend told me. As I read this old, ancient, and "outdated" book it began to change my young, ignorant, and modern perception about who was behind the story. I realized I wasn't reading it . . . it was reading me. It was a story like no other story. It was a story written by the Author of Life. It offered significance. This story changed history.

This story changed everything for me. This story will also change everything for Gen Z.

INVITATION FOR THIS GENERATION

Are you looking for a silver bullet solution to reach this generation? Look no further than the word of God. Most books you will read on Gen Z will seek to find some other solution based on modern social science, trends, or general research. I want to challenge you to look to God's word as the guide to help you engage with Gen Z.

Earlier we saw how Psalm 78 acts as a model of engagement for older generations to younger generations. The older is to tell the younger the glorious deeds of the Lord (Ps 78:4)! There is no better way to do this than by walking through the Bible from beginning to end. I'm not necessarily talking about a one-year Bible reading plan, but a plan to help this generation understand the story of Scripture beginning to end. A plan to find who is really at the center of the story of history and Scripture. Gen Z must understand the story that changed history so that they may find true life.

There are three reasons why teaching and inviting Gen Z to engage with the story of Scripture from Genesis to Revelation is the most worthwhile investment of our time.

First, the story of Scripture is an unchanging story like no other. This generation is captivated by stories. If we are to change the narrative on this generation, then we must offer a better narrative, and there is none better than the Bible. God's story has impacted people from all times and all generations, and it will impact Gen Z.

Second, Gen Z is biblically illiterate. We must help this generation understand the story arc of Scripture. The Bible is not sixty-six separate books written over fifteen hundred years by forty authors who haphazardly assembled stories. The Bible is *one book with one story*, and Jesus is at the center.

The Bible can be a daunting book to read, especially when one doesn't know the flow of the story. A key reason for biblical illiteracy is that the Bible is difficult to read! No normal person picks up a 1,500-page, ancient book and expects comprehension to be a breeze. Yet if the Bible can be taught fully, regularly, and with Christ as the center, then Gen Zers can better understand the story and its relevance for their lives today.

Third, a challenge to engage with the entire story of Scripture is powerful enough to topple the shaky story of secularism. Why? God himself wrote the story and has been using his word to transform lives for thousands of years. His word brings life Gen Z so desperately needs. The story of Scripture from Genesis to Revelation is powerful for both Christians and non-Christians. It is an instrument of discipleship to form young Gen Z Christians and an instrument for evangelism. Many in this generation may believe life is found by looking within yourself. The story of Scripture reveals how God has been and will be the source of life for those who look to him. The Bible is not a book of answers about life, but it is a book focused on God, the one who gives all life.

So, let's follow the story of Scripture from Genesis to Revelation. Over the next two chapters we will see the entire story. In this chapter we will trace the story from Genesis to Jesus. In the next chapter the story will continue from Jesus to Revelation. These chapters will serve as a dual-pronged approach to seeing how

Scripture engages Gen Z with a trans-generational gospel to live a countercultural life. Let's start with the beginning of all things.

CREATION, FALL, AND PROMISE

God created all things, and he sustains all things. "In the beginning, God created the heavens and the earth" (Gen 1:1). He chose to create man and make them in his image (Gen 1:26–27). He then commissioned man to "be fruitful and multiply and fill the earth and subdue it" (Gen 1:28).

Though there was so much promise in this new creation, Adam and Eve chose to rebel against God by eating the fruit of the tree. God created mankind to be in relationship with him, but Adam and Eve's rebellion broke this relationship with God. Their sin made them guilty before a perfect, holy, and just God! They were now rebels whose hearts needed to be change, whose relationship needed to be redeemed (Gen 3:13–19).

In God's goodness, he promised a way forward. Speaking to the one who deceived Adam and Eve, the Lord said, "I will put enmity between you and the woman, and between your offspring and her offspring; he shall bruise your head, and you shall bruise his heel" (Gen 3:15). There will be an offspring from Adam and Eve who will overcome the evil one! Who will be the offspring who will bruise the enemy's head? Who will overcome the enemy?

NOAH

Fast-forward a couple of generations, and we learn that the rebels and rebellion have multiplied. Genesis 6:5 says, "The Lord saw that the wickedness of man was great in the earth, and every intention of the thoughts of his heart was only evil continually." Because of their wickedness, the Lord planned to blot out mankind from the land with a flood. But one man, named Noah, found favor in the Lord's eyes.

The Lord tells Noah that he will flood the earth to blot man out, but Noah should build an ark to keep him, his family, and creatures alive. Noah is obedient, builds the ark, and continues to find favor in the Lord's eyes.

In Genesis chapters 8–9, God covenants with Noah. The Lord promises Noah he will not blot man off the face of the earth again. No matter how wicked and sinful the rebels become, he will keep his covenant. The sign of the Lord's covenant was a rainbow. A covenant is a relational promise. God makes covenants with people. He chooses to work with people to bring about his good plans.

But the flood and the promise made to Noah did not fix man's problem. Just two chapters later, in Genesis 11, man desired to build a tower to make their name great, not the name of the one who had created them. Once again the people sinned and rebelled. So, the Lord confused the language of these people and scattered them across the earth. How will the Lord redeem all people who are scattered across the earth?

ABRAHAM

In Genesis 12, another man found favor in the Lord's eyes. The Lord called Abraham to leave all he knew and go to a land the Lord would show. The Lord made a promise to Abraham to bless him, to make his name great, and through him to bless all the families of the earth (Gen 12:1–3). This promise was amplified and repeated as a covenant to Abraham two different times (Gen 15:1–21; 17:1–14).

Abraham's call and covenant are foundational to the story of Scripture. Through Abraham, God promises land, offspring, and blessing for his people. These promises of land, offspring, and blessing are driving themes throughout the entire story. How will these promises impact the rest of the story?

Moses and the Law

As the story continues, we see the Lord repeat the promise of Abraham to his son Isaac and his grandson Jacob. Jacob was later renamed Israel, the name all of God's people would be called. As Jacob neared the end of his life, he and his family made their way to Egypt. Israel would live in Egypt and later become enslaved for four hundred years.

In the book of Exodus, we see the Lord use Moses and his brother Aaron to convince Pharaoh, the king of Egypt, to let God's people go to worship him. The event of God's people leaving Egypt is known as the exodus and was a pivotal moment in the history of Israel. It showed that the Lord rescues and the Lord keeps his promises.

When the people of Israel came out of Egypt, they came to Mount Sinai, where the Lord made another covenant with them. The Lord promised to make them his treasured possession among all peoples. They would be a kingdom of priests and a holy nation if they obeyed his voice (Exod 19:1–8). The Lord clarified further what they should obey, laying out the law and the Ten Commandments (Exod 20:1–21).

Growing up, I heard the Ten Commandments and I always likened them to the rules at the pool—rules set in place just to ruin the fun. No running, no jumping, no diving, no fun. Why would God do this if he is good?

Yet, I hope we can see how the Lord was doing something altogether different here. He was creating a people; he was crafting a story! The law was meant to make God's people Israel a light to the world around them. When they lived differently, the world would take notice, and this honored the Lord (Deut 4:5–6). Would Israel keep the law and be a light to the world?

Israel and the Land

Though Moses instructed the people to abide by the law, it became clear they could not. The people refused to obey God's voice and could not keep his instructions. The rebels continued to rebel against God! The result of the peoples' disobedience was forty years of wandering in the desert. The older, disbelieving generation of Israel would die before the rest went to the promised land of Canaan. The Lord entrusted entering the land to the next generation.

At the end of Israel's desert wandering, Moses died, and the mantle of leadership was passed to Joshua. The book of Joshua recounts the story of Israel entering, taking the land of Canaan, and beginning to settle the land. In Judges, we learn that the people failed to conquer the land the way God commanded and continued to live as rebels. As a result of their continued rebellion, the Lord raised up judges to rule over the people of Israel. In Samuel, the people decided they wanted to be like other nations and have a king. Saul became the first king of Israel and ultimately disobeyed the Lord. He was a rebel king, just like his disobedient people. So, there was still a core problem: the people were rebels with rebel hearts; how could they become a holy nation? How could they obey the Lord?

DAVID

Just like before, the Lord's favor fell on one man: David. He became king over Israel, and the Lord established a covenant with him. In the covenant, the Lord promised to raise up a son of David to build a temple for the Lord. He also promised to David a son who would establish the throne of David's kingdom forever (2 Sam 7:13).

David's son Solomon did indeed build a temple for the Lord. It became clear that Solomon was not the king whose throne would be established forever. After Solomon died, the kingdom of Israel was divided into the Northern Kingdom and the Southern Kingdom, both of which were ruled by kings who were a shadow of King David.

Israel's history continued in the same pattern. The people transgressed the Lord's covenants, and the Lord raised up judges, kings, or prophets to call the people to repentance. But the questions continued unanswered: Who would obey the Lord? Who was the offspring of Abraham? Who was this king who would rule forever?

THE PROPHETS AND THE NEW COVENANT

The prophets, Isaiah though Malachi, shed more light on the state of Israel's predicament. The prophet Isaiah told of the people's hard, rebellious hearts and their need of repentance because judgment was coming. Isaiah and Jeremiah warned the people that the Lord would strip them of their land, and they would be exiled. And it happened. Israel was taken by enemy people to a foreign land. Prophets like Ezekiel and Daniel prophesied to the people of Israel from captivity. Though the people would eventually return to the land of Israel, it all seemed to be a shadow of its former glory.

Though the prophets spoke judgment on the people, they also offered hope. God was faithful, even when his people were unfaithful. He would keep the covenant promise made to Abraham and David. The hope came through a message of a new, everlasting covenant—a covenant of peace.

The new covenant was not like the other covenants. In this covenant, the Lord would put his law in the people (Jer 31:31–34). In this covenant, the Lord promised he would give people a new heart (Ezek 34:36–37). Alongside this future promise, the Lord reaffirmed the covenant with David. The Lord promised there would be a day when a new David would be a shepherd and prince over his people (Ezek 34:23–24).

The Old Testament ends with lingering questions. How will God keep his promises? Who is the offspring of Adam who will overcome the enemy? Who will establish the new covenant? Who is the Shepherd, Prince, and King from the line of David?

GEN Z AND THE STORY SO FAR

We live in a binge culture, a culture obsessed with the next story, the next star, the next TV show. In the world of steaming TV shows, any episode worth watching ends on a cliff-hanger, with unanswered questions. Each season ends with even larger questions. We are drawn to the progression of the characters, to the development of the plot. The peak and the climax of the story is what everyone wants to see; it's why we binge. We want the answers to all the lingering questions. Yet, in TV shows the apex rarely delivers. That's why we go to the next episode, to chase the next high.

The peak only delivers if we understand the impact of the story so far. Let's review the story to see how different aspects of the broad arc of Scripture impact Gen Z.

Creation teaches us that mankind is not a cosmic accident; we are created by an intentional and loving God who created us to bear his image to the world. Sin shows us how mankind rebelled and continues to rebel against God. Sin broke our relationship with God, others, and ourselves. God's promise to Adam and Eve in Genesis 3 reveals to us that despite mankind's sin, he will provide a way of escape. The story of Noah and the flood explains that sin has real consequences and that the Lord will keep the promises he's made to his people. All of these are core truths that we cannot shy away from, no matter how unpopular they may be in Gen Z's secular worldview.

God's promise to Abraham once again shows God's faithfulness to sinful people. In fact, God's faithfulness is so consistent, Gen Z can use Gen 12:1–3 as a pattern to understand the rest of the story of Scripture. Moses, Israel, and the law confirms how God protects and keeps his people. The law invites God's people to live counterculturally as priests representing him to the world.

David and the kings following teach us how God is keeping his promise to raise up a redeemer, even as his people are sinful. Gen Z can find hope in these promises. The prophets instruct this generation in the tension between judgment and hope. Gen Z cares deeply for the causes and injustices in this world, but the Lord *will* make all things right. Gen Z lacks hope in the difficulties of life today, but the Lord promises he will offer hope through keeping his promises.

The story so far shows Gen Zers that they are not a cosmic accident. They are created by a loving God who is intricately involved in the world. He is a God who is compassionate and gracious, wanting all to know him. Now let's answer all those lingering questions.

JESUS: THE CENTER OF THE STORY

The first verse of the New Testament says: "The book of the genealogy of Jesus Christ, the son of David, the son of Abraham" (Matt 1:1). From the beginning, the New Testament writers want readers to understand that the entire story of the Old Testament is pointing to Jesus! Jesus is the offspring of Abraham. Jesus comes from David. Jesus will crush the head of the enemy. It's all about Jesus.

Just as the story of Scripture finds life in Jesus, so too should Gen Z. Jesus answers all the questions of the Old Testament. He answers all the questions of life today. Where can I find life? Where do I find purpose? What is truth? How will I be satisfied? All of these questions find their answer in Jesus.

The Gospels, Matthew, Mark, Luke, and John, depict the same Jesus, but with a unique lens from the author. Matthew presents Jesus as the Jewish Messiah. Mark presents Jesus as the suffering Son of God. Luke presents Jesus as the savior for all people. John presents Jesus as the eternal Son who reveals the Father.[1]

So, Jesus, the offspring of Abraham, the offspring of David, was born of a virgin. He lived a perfect life as he "increased in wisdom and in stature and in favor with God and man" (Luke 2:52). When he was around thirty years old he began a ministry lasting three years. He taught about the kingdom of God, called people to repent, healed people of diseases, and asked disciples to follow him. Ultimately, he was betrayed by one of his closest disciples and was crucified at the hands of the Jewish religious leaders. Jesus was not the Messiah the people wanted, but he was the Messiah the story of Scripture foretold.

1. Strauss, *Four Portraits, One Jesus*, 30.

At least three times, Jesus told his disciples he would be delivered over to the religious leaders and put to death. He also foretold he would rise on the third day (Mark 8:31; 9:31; 10:34). Jesus was put to death on the cross as a sacrifice for the sins of the world. He then rose from the dead to show victory over death and authority over all things. All of these things happened according to the Scriptures (Luke 24:27; 1 Cor 15:3-4). This is the good news of the gospel!

The good news is this: God saves sinners through Jesus. Sinners are saved by grace through faith in the finished work of Jesus (Eph 2:8-9). Jesus covers our sins past, present, and future. We are forgiven. We were unrighteous rebels, but now we have righteousness from Christ. In John 14:6, Jesus says, "I am the way, and the truth, and the life. No one comes to the Father except through me." In Jesus, God ends our rebellion through his covenantal love.

How are we to respond to this news? How are we to respond to Jesus as the apex of the story of Scripture?

If you are a Christian, you should praise God! Praise the Lord for his goodness to his people. Praise the Lord for his faithfulness to keep his word and to redeem people to know him. Then, share this good news with everyone!

If you are not a Christian, the response is different. Your response is to repent and believe in the gospel! Repent, or turn from your sinful ways. Repentance means acknowledging you are totally unable to save yourself or produce a perfect, righteous life. Repentance means throwing yourself on the goodness of God to save you. Next, you are to believe! Believe the good news of new life found in Jesus' life, death, resurrection, and ascension. Believe Jesus paid the price for your sin and died as a sacrifice in your place. Our response to this news is to acknowledge our sin, turn from our sinful ways, and trust in the finished work of Jesus!

Generation Z's greatest need is the gospel. The gospel is the trans-generational message every single person needs to hear. This news destroys the lies of today's world. The world says you create and believe in your own truth. The world says to look within yourself to find life. None of those things will satisfy. Life does not come from what we do. It comes from what Jesus did. Life is not about what we accomplish, but it's about what Jesus accomplished and is accomplishing.

A STORY FOR THE NEXT GENERATION

Recently some friends and I went to a park near my house and struck up a gospel conversation with two members of Gen Z named Landon and Hannah. They were both sitting at a picnic table with headphones in and looking at their phones. They were both eighteen years old and had moved to Portland from West Virginia for a fresh start in life.

Initially, Landon seemed uninterested in our conversation. But as the conversation turned spiritual, Landon began to dig his heels in and push back on the good news of Jesus. He said he grew up in an atheistic household that was antagonistic to any organized religion. Yet, at the same time as he dug his heels in, he dug deeper into the conversation. He began to ask questions about the Bible and the church.

Most of Landon's hang-ups in our conversation were pointed either directly at Christians or the Bible. He had questions on the historicity of Noah and the ark, or Jonah and the whale. He couldn't believe that God would let such immorality reign in the world—especially in places like the Catholic Church. He disagreed that people are born sinful. Yet, he agreed nobody was perfect. He had questions on human rights, morality, and justice.

As we talked more, I realized Landon had many questions on these topics but had never actually talked to Christians about these questions. All of his thoughts on religion seemed to come from YouTube videos and online memes. He was confused on what the Old and New Testament were. He had no frame of reference for the entire story. He reduced Christians to people who do bad things that they think are good and the Bible to a crazy story these Christians believe.

Yet, by the end of the conversation, Landon said, "Wow, I like a lot of your answers. I think I disagree right now, but all of your answers are so consistent." Why were they consistent? Because my friends and I all went to the same source: God's word. We did not answer his questions with feelings or what we thought Landon wanted to hear. We answered with what God's word says and how each of these questions points to Jesus.

My conversation with Landon reminds me of so many conversations with Gen Z. This generation has question, deep questions, about God, life, and their purpose in this world. But they do not have the tools to answer those questions other than a search on Google and a quick look on social media. There is a gap between Gen Z and God's word. Our role should be to bridge the gap!

When interacting with Generation Z, we should share the entire story of Scripture. Do not compromise on the core truths in Scripture. Do not neglect to proclaim the gospel. Our role is to be faithful to God's word and compassionate to the people we interact with. We cannot change hearts; only God can do that.

The story of Scripture is a story like no other. It is a story a biblically illiterate generation needs to hear. And it's a story strong enough to topple the shaky foundation of secularism and a life built on expressive individualism. Technology will not answer Gen Z's deepest questions, but God's word will.

I believe God wants to reach the Landons of today. The first and greatest need of Gen Z is the gospel. The gospel shared from Genesis to Revelation is a powerful tool to do this. The gospel not only saves this generation, but it can also transform the way members of Gen Z live. Let's look at the rest of the story and see how Scripture teaches us to live a countercultural life.

REFLECTION: BRIDGING THE GAP

1. Ask yourself, what hard questions about Scripture have I neglected out of protection for Gen Z?

2. Ask Gen Zers whether they feel like they understand the story of Scripture. What are questions they have or gaps that

need to be filled? What are the big questions their friends ask that they don't have answers to?

3. Ask Gen Zers if they have repented of their sins and trusted Jesus. What impact has this made on their day-to-day lives?

9

A Countercultural Narrative

WHILE TRAVELING IN THE Northeast, I met a campus ministry leader at a well-known school. The ministry leader told me about the momentum of the ministry and that they had recently seen a student accept Christ. He continued to share that their ministry would celebrate anytime someone became a Christian.

I remember asking him, "What do you do to celebrate?"

He replied, "We go to a thrift store and buy an old wooden chair. Then, we gather people from our ministry, and someone smashes the chair to pieces to celebrate that someone came to know Christ!" Smashing the chair symbolizes that their old life is gone and there is no going back. They are now seated in the new chair, next to the king! They call it a "chair smash." It's how they celebrate at the salvation of a friend.

Chair smash? What an epic and beautiful idea. This ministry made it their habit to celebrate the miracle of new life. Actually, I would say they celebrate two miracles. First, they celebrate someone's new life in Christ. Second, they celebrate a young college student's evangelistic efforts. Both of these are miracles!

In today's secular age, and among the least religious demographic in US history, this ministry is in the business of miracles. They see Gen Z students sharing their faith and Gen Z students responding to the gospel. The story of Christ crucified for the sins of the world is not an old story for older generations, it is a story for the misfits of Gen Z. They dream to change the narrative for this generation.

This ministry's celebration of the two miracles follows a pattern in the story of Scripture. Where the last chapter saw Jesus as the answer to all the lingering questions of the Old Testament, this chapter will see the impact of Jesus on the lives of those who call him Lord and savior. From Jesus' resurrection to the end of all things in Revelation, Christians are to live differently as a result of the finished work of Christ. They are to be witnesses of Jesus' life, death, and resurrection to the world. They are to live differently in fellowship with other Christians through the church. They are also to live differently than the world around them when it comes to where they set their hope: the new heavens and the new earth. The gospel launches Christians into a countercultural life. And many in Gen Z are prepared to be misfits for the cause of Christ in the world.

WITNESSES

Luke is the author of both the Gospel of Luke and the book of Acts. As one author he links together his two pieces of the story of Jesus and the early church in a powerful way. He displays the dual miracles of Jesus saving his followers and commissioning them out for action. At the end of his gospel account, he shares some of Jesus' final words with his disciples before he ascends to heaven:

> "These are my words that I spoke to you while I was still with you, *that everything written about me in the Law of Moses and the Prophets and the Psalms must be fulfilled.*" Then he opened their minds to understand the Scriptures, and said to them, "Thus it is written, that the *Christ should suffer and on the third day rise from the dead, and that repentance for the forgiveness of sins should be proclaimed in his name to all nations,* beginning from Jerusalem. *You are witnesses of these things.* And behold, I am sending the promise of my Father upon you. But

stay in the city until you are clothed with power from on high." (Luke 24:44–49, emphasis added)

Two observations are key to grasp here. First, Jesus fulfills all that was written about him in the Law, the Prophets, and the Psalms. Through his death and resurrection, he offers forgiveness of sins through repentance. Second, Jesus' disciples are to be witnesses of these things! The good news of Jesus, as shown through the entire story of Scripture, is good news for everyone. Those who follow Jesus are to make him known by being witnesses.

The apostle Paul speaks to the same dual reality in 2 Cor 5:17–21. First, we are new creations. Second, we are ambassadors of Christ to the world. This is one identity as a Christian, not two separate identities. In Christ we are both new creations and ambassadors to the world around us—and the world is watching!

This mission to witness is repeated at the beginning of the book of Acts, which chronicles the start and growth of the early church at the hands of Peter, the apostles, and the apostle Paul. Jesus' final words before ascending to the Father are, "But you will receive power when the Holy Spirit has come upon you, and you will be my witnesses in Jerusalem and in all Judea and Samaria, and to the end of the earth" (Acts 1:8).

Interestingly, the book of Acts follows these geographical boundaries, seeing the gospel take root in Jerusalem (Acts 1–7), then spread to Judea and Samaria (Acts 8–9), and then to the ends of the earth (Acts 10–28). The gospel is going global by the hands of the early church.

In Matt 28, Jesus gives a similar commission, which is very instructive for Christians today:

> "All authority in heaven and on earth has been given
> to me. Go therefore and make disciples of all nations,
> baptizing them in the name of the Father and of the Son
> and of the Holy Spirit, teaching them to observe all that
> I have commanded you. And behold, I am with you al-
> ways, to the end of the age." (Matt 28:18–20)

Since God's promise to Abraham in Gen 12, he has desired to see all the families of the earth blessed. Now Jesus tells his disciples that their mission is to make disciples, baptize, and teach all the peoples of the earth. God's heart for the world is clear, beginning in the Old Testament, and now the marching orders are even clearer from Jesus.

Luke 24, Acts 1, and Matt 28 all shape the mission of the church today. The invitation Jesus gives to his people is to make disciples of all nations! The church is God's chosen method to reach the world. The Christian life is one of becoming a new creation in Christ and awaiting the new creation spoken about in Revelation.

This should impact the way older generations think about their role in reaching and discipling Gen Z. For the members of Gen Z who are Christians, this mission for the church is their mission! Tell them the risk is worth it. Tell them how a lack of the knowledge of Jesus is the greatest injustice in the world. Tell them to use their dreams and vocations for the glory of God in their home nation and to the ends of the earth. Share this vision to be countercultural witnesses and change the narrative.

THE CHURCH

Implicit in Acts and the rest of the New Testament is the growth of the church. The church grows in Acts, and the rest of the New Testament bears witness to this growth through various epistles written to churches across the Roman Empire.

In Matt 16:18, after Peter confesses Jesus as the Messiah, Jesus says to Peter, "And I tell you, you are Peter, and on this rock I will build my church, and the gates of hell shall not prevail against it." This is the first direct mention of the church in the New Testament. Throughout the rest of the New Testament, the church begins to spread across the world by the hands of the apostles. The church should be of utmost important to all Christians, including Gen Z Christians. The pastor and founder of the 9Marks movement, Mark Dever says,

The church should be regarded as important to Christians because of its importance to Christ. Christ founded the church (Matt 16:18), purchased it with his blood (Acts 20:28), and intimately identifies himself with it (Acts 9:4). The church is the body of Christ (1 Cor 12:12, 27; Eph 1:22–23; 4:12; 5:20–30; Col 1:18, 24; 3:15), the dwelling place of his saints (1 Cor 3:16–17; Eph 2:18, 22; 4:4), and the chief instrument for glorifying God in the world (Ezek 36:22–38; Eph 3:10). Finally, the church is God's instrument for bringing both the gospel to the nations and a great host of redeemed humanity to himself (Luke 24:46–48; Rev 5:9).[1]

He goes on to summarize, "The church is the gospel made visible."[2] Meaning, Christians are to audibly preach the gospel as witnesses. They are also to make the gospel visible by the way they live, love, and worship. The church is a countercultural institution in today's world.

Gen Z, like every generation, will have problems with the church. The church is made up of imperfect sinners who need the grace of God in the gospel. So, it should be of no surprise that there is sin, hypocrisy, false teaching, and embezzlement. For many, it can be easy to judge the church from the outside, without doing the hard work of trying to be what Jesus called us to be.

Even though Jesus came and conquered sin and death, the hope of the renewal of all things is not complete. We live in the tension of Christ's finished work on the cross and his second coming. In this waiting, we are to gather with other Christians in a local assembly, loving one another in a countercultural way. Christians cannot follow Jesus alone; they need the church. A church is not two people reading the Bible, or a podcast, or a church app.

We must help Gen Zers see the importance of the church. We must help them see the importance of cross-generational relationships and wisdom. We do this by teaching clearly on the church and the importance of the church in God's eyes. And ultimately,

1. Dever, *The Church*, xi.
2. Dever, *The Church*, xi.

the church is the hope in the world, pointing to the greater hope in new creation.

New Creation: A New Hope

The Bible concludes with a picture of the end of all things. It is glorious and hopeful. The New Testament finishes with Revelation, which is a series of visions from John that constitute a message for the church today, and it is a picture of the final days to come. In Rev 7:9–10 we see a glimpse of who will be in heaven and who they are worshiping:

> After this I looked, and behold, a great multitude that no one could number, from every nation, from all tribes and peoples and languages, standing before the throne and before the Lamb, clothed in white robes, with palm branches in their hands, and crying out with a loud voice, "Salvation belongs to our God who sits on the throne, and to the Lamb!"

Not only is there a diversity of people worshiping God from every nation, tribe, people, and language, but there is the renewal of all things. The last two chapters of the Bible reveal a stunning picture of new creation. Just as the story of Scripture *begins with creation* in Genesis, Revelation shows how the story *ends with a new creation.*

The new creation is a new heaven and a new earth. Now, the dwelling place of God is with man (Rev 21:3). The effects of the fall are removed and there will be no mourning, nor crying, nor pain (Rev 21:4–5). The story of Scripture is indeed one story with *Jesus* at the center. Putting our hope in Jesus above anything else is countercultural.

A Collision of Narratives

We've seen the countercultural message of witness, church, and new creation in the New Testament. But the question is, how does the narrative of Scripture speak directly to the narrative of Gen Z? How does God's narrative inform their narrative? We must embrace the collision of these narratives.

The narrative of Scripture from Genesis to Revelation, and God's desire for his people to know him and grow as disciples, will shape Gen Zers in unique ways. The Lord desires to use their distinctive upbringing, worldview, and motivations for his glory.

First, let's recap what we know about Gen Zers and their story. This promising generation is composed of about seventy million people born between 1995 and 2012. We know the world they live in has impacted their motivations. While specific defining moments such as the Great Recession and the COVID-19 pandemic shaped Gen Z's childhood and worldview, so did societal trends like changing definitions on gender and sexuality, divided politics, and decreased religious activity.

Gen Z has grown up in a secular world that is post-Christian, post-truth, and completely obsessed with the individual. Where secularism may be the worldview of Gen Zers, technology gives them the tools to live this worldview out. Gen Z grew up in a world with limitless content on the internet and limitless connections through social media. The smartphone and all of its content and connection is in their pockets.

Gen Z has grown up in a time when the very definition of growing up is changing. All of these aspects influence Gen Zers' worldview and motivations. They are motivated by connection, caution, causes, and customization. Yet, at the same time, this generation is deeply anxious, lonely, and depressed. This is the narrative of Gen Z.

The narrative of Scripture comes alongside and shapes the narrative of Gen Z. The greatest hope anyone can offer Gen Z is the trans-generational hope found in Christ alone. When Gen Zers find their hope in Jesus, they are invited to live a countercultural life that reshapes the narrative their peers are living.

The church is the countercultural institution in today's world. It dismantles the selfish focus of expressive individualism in exchange for loving one another. The word of God is a countercultural tool against the uses of today's technology. We are not all-knowing, but the Lord provides exactly what we need in his word. The hope of new creation is the conclusion to the countercultural narrative of Scripture. Today's world offers little in the way of hope, but God offers hope in a renewal of all things.

The Lord can also direct, correct, and use all four primary motivations of Gen Z.

Connection: God desires that his people connect with other believers in a local church and with nonbelievers, sharing the gospel to the ends of the earth. God can leverage Gen Z's desire to connect through social media by changing it from a platform of self-promotion to a platform for countercultural, Christ-exalting Christian life.

Caution: Following Jesus is a risk in today's secular world. It is a risk to Gen Zers' relationships and goals and life. It may also be a risk to their comfort as one thinks of taking the gospel to the ends of the earth. But Christian members of Gen Z will see Christ's cause in the world as a risk worth taking. The Lord can use their discernment and practicality to strategically invest their lives.

Causes: God is just and merciful. Gen Z's desire to promote and invest in causes in today's world is a great area for the Lord to work. Think of how a Christian member of Gen Z could bring civility and compassion to the tension about social justice issues today. Think of how Christ's causes in the world could be promoted on social media instead of the next hot cause today.

Customization: Gen Z's desire to curate and customize is an area of growth for them. As Gen Zers mature in faith, the Lord will give them opportunities to sacrifice in order to serve others rather than their own curated desires. In fact, the Lord may enable them to connect well with people by desiring to serve them uniquely rather than serve themselves. Customized service may be a great way to outdo one another in love.

SMASHING MELONS

In 2019, after hearing about the dual miracle of the "chair smash," I wanted to do something similar. That summer I had the opportunity to host a summer discipleship program in Southern California with over twenty-five students from fifteen universities around the US. The students gathered together for the purpose of growing in evangelism, discipleship, Bible study, cultural study, and cross-cultural missions.

Every summer, one of the most daunting aspects of each week was evangelism. Each Saturday we would send out students two-by-two to go door-to-door and share the gospel with complete strangers. Can you imagine as an eighteen-year-old being told to go knock on someone's door and share the gospel with them? Yeah, they were terrified too.

By the end of the first Saturday, the students felt confident knocking on doors but still felt the daunting pressure of sharing the gospel with strangers. By week two, the group felt more comfortable sharing the gospel. By the third week, something incredible happened. One of the pairs of students knocked on a door, prayed for the woman who answered, shared the gospel with her, and she accepted Christ! When we reconvened as a group, this pair told the story and people lost their minds. People. Went. Crazy.

So, what did we do? We took the cold, Northeastern tradition of a chair smash and gave it a California summer flare. We called it a "melon smash." We went and purchased a watermelon and told the pair who shared the gospel to go up on the fourth-floor balcony and throw it off in celebration. Then we had a massive dance party to celebrate. That summer we smashed three more watermelons by God's grace.

This moment of melon smash is the beautiful mixture of everything we've covered in the last two chapters. The gospel is the trans-generational message Gen Z needs to hear and the message Gen Z Christians must share. The Christian life is an invitation to live counterculturally by doing crazy things like sharing the gospel and smashing watermelons.

Moments like this are not a formula. I cannot provide an easy, five-step process to recreate something similar at your church or in your ministry. But what I can tell you is the Lord desires that the next generation come to know him. And when people meet Jesus, their lives change.

As parents, be guides to your children. Don't tell them to follow their hearts and become the best version of themselves. Share biblical wisdom rather than worldly wisdom.

As grandparents, seek to connect with your grandchildren though they may be absorbed in their phones. Don't drive a wedge between you and them with "back in my day" stories.

Pastors and ministry workers, invest in the youth of today! Invest in the youth ministry. Dive deep on the entire story of Scripture from Genesis to Revelation to answer the hard questions this generation is facing. If they don't get it from your teaching, ministry, or church, then they will seek answers to the questions in other places.

And for everyone else: "We urge you, brothers, admonish the idle, encourage the fainthearted, help the weak, be patient with them all" (1 Thess 5:14).

Don't discount what the Lord can do through this promising generation of misfits and dreamers. Move from misunderstanding to understanding. Bridge the gap. Develop a heart of compassion and change the narrative for Gen Z. There are more melons to be smashed!

Yeet.

REFLECTION: BRIDGING THE GAP

1. Ask yourself, in what ways can you celebrate the spiritual growth of Gen Z?

2. Ask Gen Zers what they think of evangelism and missions in the Christian life.

3. Ask Gen Zers whether they are involved in a local church. In what ways is this involvement important (or unimportant)?

APPENDIX

Further Reading by Topic

PERSPECTIVE ON GEN Z

The Connected Generation: How Christian Leaders around the World Can Strengthen Faith and Well-Being among 18–35-Year-Olds. Barna Group and World Vision International, 2019.

Elmore, Tim, and Andrew McPeak. *Generation Z Unfiltered: Facing Nine Hidden Challenges of the Most Anxious Population.* Atlanta: Poet Gardner, 2019.

Gen Z: The Culture, Beliefs and Motivations Shaping the Next Generation; A Barna Report Produced in Partnership with Impact 360 Institute. Barna Group, 2018.

Gen Z: Vol 2. Barna Group, 2020.

McDowell, Sean, and Sean McDowell. *So the Next Generation Will Know: Preparing Young Christians for a Challenging World.* Colorado Springs: David C. Cook, 2019.

White, James Emery. *Meet Generation Z: Understanding and Reaching the New Post-Christian World.* Grand Rapids: Baker, 2017.

General Perspective on Gen Z

Fromm, Jeff, and Angie Read. *Marketing to Gen Z: The Rules for Reaching This Vast and Very Different Generation of Influencers.* New York: AMACOM, 2018.

Lukianoff, Greg, and Jonathan Haidt. *The Coddling of the American Mind: How Good Intentions and Bad Ideas Are Setting Up a Generation for Failure.* New York: Penguin, 2018.

Seemiller, Corey, and Meghan Grace. *Generation Z: A Century in the Making.* Abingdon, UK: Routledge, Taylor & Francis, 2019.

————. *Generation Z Goes to College.* San Francisco: Jossey-Bass, 2016.

————. *Generation Z Leads: A Guide for Developing the Leadership Capacity of Generation Z Students.* North Charleston, SC: CreateSpace, 2017.

Stillman, David, and Jonah Stillman. *Gen Z @ Work: How the Next Generation Is Transforming the Workplace.* 1st ed. New York: Harper Business, 2017.

Twenge, Jean M. *iGen: Why Today's Super-Connected Kids Are Growing Up Less Rebellious, More Tolerant, Less Happy—and Completely Unprepared for Adulthood—and What That Means for the Rest of Us.* New York: Atria, 2018.

Secularism

Hansen, Collin. *Our Secular Age: Ten Years of Reading and Applying Charles Taylor.* Deerfield, IL: Gospel Coalition, 2017.

Smith, James K. A. *How (Not) to Be Secular: Reading Charles Taylor.* Grand Rapids: Eerdmans, 2014.

Taylor, Charles. *A Secular Age.* Cambridge, MA: Belknap, 2007.

Trueman, Carl R. *The Rise and Triumph of the Modern Self: Cultural Amnesia, Expressive Individualism, and the Road to Sexual Revolution.* Wheaton: Crossway, 2020.

Technology

Fernandez, Luke, and Susan J. Matt. *Bored, Lonely, Angry, Stupid: Changing Feelings about Technology, from the Telegraph to Twitter.* Cambridge, MA: Harvard University Press, 2019.

Reinke, Tony. *12 Ways Your Phone Is Changing You.* Wheaton: Crossway, 2017.

———. *God, Technology, and the Christian Life.* Wheaton: Crossway, 2022.

Changing the Narrative

Dever, Mark. *The Church: The Gospel Made Visible.* 9Marks. Nashville: B&H Academic, 2012.

Kinnaman, David, and Mark Matlock. *Faith for Exiles: 5 Ways for a New Generation to Follow Jesus in Digital Babylon.* Grand Rapids: Baker, 2019.

Lawrence, Michael. *Biblical Theology in the Life of the Church: A Guide for Ministry.* Wheaton: Crossway, 2010.

Sayers, Mark. *Disappearing Church: From Cultural Relevance to Gospel Resilience.* Chicago: Moody, 2016.

———. *Reappearing Church: The Hope for Renewal in the Rise of Our Post-Christian Culture.* Chicago: Moody, 2019.

Translating the Great Commission: What Spreading the Gospel Means to U.S. Christians in the 21st Century. Barna Group and Seed Company, 2018.

Bibliography

Alter, Charlotte, et al. "Greta Thunberg Is TIME's 2019 Person of the Year." *Time*, n.d. https://time.com/person-of-the-year-2019-greta-thunberg/.

Casteel, Tim. "Frozen 2: The Terrible Freedom of Writing Your Own Script—Tim Casteel." Timcasteel.com (blog), Nov 30, 2019. https://web.archive.org/web/20210421200010/https://www.timcasteel.com/2019/11/frozen-2-the-terrible-freedom-of-writing-your-own-script/.

Chavez, Alva. "Gimme the Stimmy! Gen Z Tells How They'll Spend the Money." *YR Media* (blog), Mar 18, 2021. https://yr.media/news/stimulus-gen-z-matt-harvey-nyla-brown-noah-johnson-alva-chavez/.

Covenant Eyes. "Porn Stats." N.d. https://www.covenanteyes.com/pornstats/.

Dever, Mark. *The Church: The Gospel Made Visible*. 9Marks. Nashville: B&H Academic, 2012.

"Generation." Merriam-Webster. Accessed Mar 27, 2022. https://www.merriam-webster.com/dictionary/generation.

Gen Z: The Culture, Beliefs and Motivations Shaping the Next Generation; A Barna Report Produced in Partnership with Impact 360 Institute. Barna Group, 2018.

Gen Z: Vol 2. Barna Group, 2020.

Golding, Bruce. "Wayfair Product Listings Spark Child Trafficking Conspiracy Theory." *New York Post*, Jul 10, 2020. https://nypost.com/2020/07/10/wayfair-product-listings-spark-child-trafficking-theory/.

Kinnaman, David, and Mark Matlock. *Faith for Exiles: 5 Ways for a New Generation to Follow Jesus in Digital Babylon*. Grand Rapids: Baker, 2019.

Lukianoff, Greg, and Jonathan Haidt. *The Coddling of the American Mind: How Good Intentions and Bad Ideas Are Setting Up a Generation for Failure*. New York: Penguin, 2018.

Meade, Aimee. "'Philanthroteens': Young People Who Use Their Pocket Money to Change the World." *The Guardian*, Jun 19, 2015. https://www.theguardian.com/voluntary-sector-network/2015/jun/19/philanthroteens-young-people-who-use-their-pocket-money-to-change-the-world.

"Number of Monthly Active Facebook Users Worldwide as of 4th Quarter 2021." Statista. Accessed Mar 27, 2022. https://www.statista.com/statistics/264810/number-of-monthly-active-facebook-users-worldwide/.

"Online Use in 1996." Pew Research Center, Dec 16, 1996. https://www.pewresearch.org/politics/1996/12/16/online-use/.

Perrin, Andrew, and Monica Anderson. "Share of U.S. Adults Using Social Media, Including Facebook, Is Mostly Unchanged Since 2018." *Pew Research Center*, Apr 10, 2019. https://www.pewresearch.org/fact-tank/2019/04/10/share-of-u-s-adults-using-social-media-including-facebook-is-mostly-unchanged-since-2018/.

"Porn in the Digital Age: New Research Reveals 10 Trends." Barna.com, Apr 16, 2016. https://www.barna.com/research/porn-in-the-digital-age-new-research-reveals-10-trends/.

Reinke, Tony. *12 Ways Your Phone Is Changing You*. Wheaton: Crossway, 2017.

Ronson, Jon. "How One Stupid Tweet Blew Up Justine Sacco's Life." *The New York Times*, Feb 12, 2015. https://www.nytimes.com/2015/02/15/magazine/how-one-stupid-tweet-ruined-justine-saccos-life.html.

Rosenblatt, Kalhan. "'How Dare You!' Greta Thunberg Lambasts World Leaders at U.N." *NBC News*, Sep 23, 2019. https://www.nbcnews.com/news/world/teen-climate-activist-greta-thunberg-delivers-scathing-speech-u-n-n1057621.

Sayers, Mark. *Disappearing Church: From Cultural Relevance to Gospel Resilience*. Chicago: Moody, 2016.

Schmidt, Samantha. "1 in 6 Gen Z Adults Are LGBT. And This Number Could Continue to Grow." *Washington Post*, Feb 14, 2021. https://www.washingtonpost.com/dc-md-va/2021/02/24/gen-z-lgbt/.

Seemiller, Corey, and Meghan Grace. *Generation Z: A Century in the Making*. Abingdon, UK: Routledge, Taylor & Francis, 2019.

Smith, James K. A. *How (Not) to Be Secular: Reading Charles Taylor*. Grand Rapids: Eerdmans, 2014.

Strauss, Mark L. *Four Portraits, One Jesus: A Survey of Jesus and the Gospels*. Grand Rapids: Zondervan, 2007.

Taylor, Charles. *A Secular Age*. Cambridge, MA: Belknap, 2007.

Twenge, Jean M. *iGen: Why Today's Super-Connected Kids Are Growing Up Less Rebellious, More Tolerant, Less Happy—and Completely Unprepared for Adulthood—and What That Means for the Rest of Us*. New York: Atria, 2018.

Wax, Trevin. "Expressive Individualism: What Is It?" *The Gospel Coalition*, Oct 16, 2018. https://www.thegospelcoalition.org/blogs/trevin-wax/expressive-individualism-what-is-it/.

White, James Emery. *Meet Generation Z: Understanding and Reaching the New Post-Christian World*. Grand Rapids: Baker, 2017.